12/02

OVERSIZE

D1410649

The Ultimate Visual Guide

LONDON, NEW YORK, MUNICH, PARIS,
MELBOURNE, DELHI

Senior Art Editor Lisa Lanzarini
Editor Rebecca Knowles
Editorial Assistant Julia March
Designer Dan Bunyan
Senior Editor Alastair Dougall
U.S. Editors Gary Werner and Margaret Parrish
Art Director Cathy Tincknell
Publishing Managers Cynthia O'Neill and Mary Atkinson
Production Nicola Torode
DTP Designer Jill Bunyan

First American edition, 2002
02 03 04 05 10 9 8 7 6 5 4 3 2 1

Published in the United States by DK Publishing Inc.,
375 Hudson Street, New York, New York 10014

© 2002 Disney Enterprises, Inc.
Page Design Copyright © Dorling Kindersley Ltd.

Monsters, Inc., *A Bug's Life*, *Finding Nemo* © Disney Enterprises, Inc./Pixar Animation Studios.
Winnie the Pooh: Based on the "Winnie the Pooh" works by A. A. Milne and E. H. Shepard. All Rights Reserved.
Oswald the Lucky Rabbit: © Universal.
"Academy Award(s) ®" and "Oscar(s) ®" and the Oscar ® statuette are registered trademarks and service marks of the
Academy of Motion Picture Arts and Sciences. The Oscar ® Statuette is also its copyrighted property.
ABC logo © ABC, Inc.
TARZAN ® Owned by Edgar Rice Burroughs, Inc. and Used by Permission.
COPYRIGHT © (1999) Edgar Rice Burroughs, Inc. and Disney Enterprises, Inc. All Rights Reserved.
Tron, *Something Wicked This Way Comes*, *The Rocketeer*, *James and the Giant Peach*, *The Santa Clause*, *Snow Dogs*, *Splash* © Walt Disney Pictures.
Golden Girls © Touchstone Pictures & Television. All Rights Reserved.
Down & Out in Beverly Hills, *Three Men and a Baby*, *Pretty Woman*, *The Insider*, *Dick Tracy* © Touchstone Pictures.
Arachnophobia, *The Joy Luck Club*, *Quiz Show* © Hollywood Pictures.
Pearl Harbor © Touchstone Pictures & Jerry Bruckheimer, Inc.
Toy Story 2 © Disney Enterprises, Inc./Pixar Animation Studios.
Original *Toy Story* Elements © Disney Enterprises, Inc.
Mr. Potato Head ® and Mrs. Potato Head ® are registered trademarks of Hasbro, Inc.
Used with permission © Hasbro, Inc. All Rights Reserved.
Slinky ® Dog © James Industries.
The Jungle Book is based on the Mowgli Stories in *The Jungle Book* and *The Second Jungle Book* by Rudyard Kipling.
101 Dalmatians & *102 Dalmatians* are based on the book *The Hundred and One Dalmatians* by Dodie Smith, published by The Viking Press.
The Rescuers and *The Rescuers Down Under* feature characters from the Disney film suggested by the books by Margery Sharp, *The Rescuers* and
Miss Bianca, published by William Collins Sons and Company.

Every attempt has been made to obtain permission to reproduce material protected by copyright. Where omissions
may have occurred, the publisher will be happy to add acknowledgment in future printings.

All rights reserved under International and Pan-American Copyright Conventions. No part of this publication
may be reproduced, stored in a retrieval system, or transmitted in any form or by any means,
electronic, mechanical, photocopying, recording, or otherwise, without prior
written permission of the copyright owner.

Published in Great Britain by Dorling Kindersley Limited.

Library of Congress Cataloging-in-Publication Data
Schroeder, Russell K.
Disney : The Ultimate Visual Guide / by Russell Schroeder.-- 1st American ed.
p. cm. -- (Ultimate Guides series)
ISBN 0-7894-8862-0
1. Walt Disney Company. I. Disney, Walt, 1901-1966. II. Title. III. Series.
PN1999.W27 S37 2002
384'.8'06579494--dc21

Color reproduction by Media Development and Printing Ltd.
Printed and bound in Italy by Mondadori.

See our complete product line at
www.dk.com

Disney

THE ULTIMATE VISUAL GUIDE

OVERSIZE

A Dorling Kindersley Book

BARIGHT PUBLIC LIBRARY
5555 S. 77th St.
Ralston, NE 68127

Contents

Foreword

The Walt Disney Company celebrated 100 Years of Magic in 2001 with the 100th anniversary of Walt Disney's birth. I have been with Disney almost a third of those hundred years. My job has given me the opportunity to document and study not only this last third of a century, but all the rest, too. The Walt Disney Archives, founded in 1970, is a repository of all of Disney's history, from the early days of Walt himself, to the latest movie, television show, and theme park attraction. For this book, we have opened our files of photographs, sheet music, posters, artwork, comic books, merchandise, awards, and other materials that graphically illustrate the history of Disney, so they could be gathered into a fun compilation of all that is Disney. Almost everyone has grown up with Disney in their lives, whether through a visit to a local movie theater, sitting down to view the Disney Channel, going to sleep clutching a stuffed Dumbo, or going on a family vacation to Walt Disney World. This book will help all those millions of people relive some of those cherished memories.

Dave Smith,
Archives Director,
The Walt Disney Company

American Dreamer

WALT DISNEY'S LIFE is often hailed as the fulfillment of the American dream, whereby a person achieves success through his own hard work and ability. Walt would indeed find success, but it was accompanied by failures and setbacks that would have caused many an individual to give up the business entirely!

The Early Years

WALT DISNEY WAS born to hardworking, middle-class parents in Chicago in 1901. His father Elias tried many ways to better the family's finances and bought a farm in Marceline, Missouri when Walt was four. Owing to Elias's poor health the farm was sold, yet Walt recalled the four years he spent there as the happiest of his life. The small-town values and atmosphere of Marceline would influence his films and theme parks.

Walt's parents Elias and Flora Disney. Walt was their fourth son.

Walt at 10 months old.

Modest beginning

In 1919 Walt got his first job as an artist, and soon set up his own company, Laugh-O-grams. It was not a success, but Walt did not give up. In 1923 he moved to Hollywood, California, where, with his brother Roy, he established a little studio making silent cartoons. It was a modest start for what was to become a major entertainment company.

Walt as a young teen in Kansas City, Missouri.

At 16, Walt was too young to fight in World War I. Instead, he joined the Red Cross and served in France as an ambulance driver.

Artist in the making

Walt showed an early talent for art, and by the age of seven he was already selling his drawings. He was also a natural entertainer, amusing his school friends with cartoons and stories. After the war, he returned to Kansas City, where his family was now living, determined to become a professional artist.

Walt's first solo enterprise, Laugh-O-grams, lasted just over a year.

Roy Disney and Walt stand in front of their first Hollywood studio location on Kingswell Avenue.

Walt's drawings appeared in his high-school magazine, The Voice.

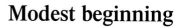

Walt at his drawing board in his early twenties.

Walt's letterhead from his early days in Kansas City as a professional cartoonist.

Oswald the Lucky Rabbit

Oswald was Walt's first successful animated character, appearing in 26 films between 1927 and 1928. He was so popular that he became the first Disney character to be merchandised, appearing on candy bars, stencil sets, and buttons. Eventually, Oswald's distributors sold the character to another studio because Walt wouldn't agree to a budget cut.

Storyboard drawings for Sleigh Bells *(1928), one of the last Oswald cartoons produced by the Disney Studio.*

OSWALD
1928

In The Fox Chase *(1928), Oswald rides on horseback to try to catch a fox.*

Oswald's appearance was, in many ways, similar to that of Walt's next creation, Mickey Mouse.

Walt (left) and Roy pose with Margie Gay, the second young actress to star in their Alice Comedies.

Alice

The Disney Brothers Studio's first series, The Alice Comedies, was based around the idea of placing Alice, played by a child actress, in an animated world. There were 56 episodes and the series was popular for several years, until audiences found the novelty wearing thin. So the Studio began its first full cartoon series, starring Oswald the Lucky Rabbit.

1924

ALICE THE PEACEMAKER

A WALT DISNEY COMIC

M.J. WINKLER DISTRIBUTOR, N.Y.

WINKLER PICTURES

Alice the Peacemaker (1924) starred Virginia Davis, who moved to California from Kansas City to appear in Disney's Alice Comedies.

Alice the Golf Bug (1927) featured Margie Gay as Alice.

1927

JOSEPH P. KENNEDY presents

ALICE THE GOLF BUG by Walt Disney

WINKLER PICTURE

An ALICE Comedy WINKLER PICTURES

DISTRIBUTED BY GREATER FBO

Enter Mickey

Plane Crazy was Mickey's first cartoon. It was animated single-handedly by Ub Iwerks.

JUST AS THE fortunes of the Disney Studio seemed to be back on track with the Oswald series, there came two devastating blows. First Walt discovered that he didn't own the rights to Oswald, and then he learned that many of his artists had been lured away to work for another studio! Walt realized he had to come up with a new cartoon character. From the desperation of the moment a new star was born—Mickey Mouse.

UB IWERKS

Walt And Mickey

From the beginning, Walt Disney provided the falsetto vocalizations for his star. He once dismissed this decision as just a cost-cutting measure. However, Walt was an instinctive actor who brought a lot of personality and charm to the role. Walt received his first Oscar® in 1932 for the creation of Mickey Mouse.

With Mickey's 10th anniversary in films approaching, the Studio produced one of his most elaborate cartoon shorts, Brave Little Tailor (1938).

Musical steamboats

To help sell the new series, a special synchronized soundtrack was added to the third Mickey film, *Steamboat Willie*. The then-revolutionary use of music helped to establish character and add comic effect. The blend of state-of-the-art technology and creativity was sensational, and the Disney Studio achieved its first real hit when *Steamboat Willie* was released on November 18, 1928.

Movie audiences, still unused to sound films, were especially delighted by Mickey's ability to make music from anything on hand, from pots and pans, to the riverboat's cargo of livestock.

An excerpt from "Steamboat Bill," the song that would lead to Mickey's stardom.

Why Willie?

Mickey first appears on the riverboat whistling the bouncy melody of the song "Steamboat Bill." The popular comedian Buster Keaton had had a recent hit with the silent movie *Steamboat Bill, Jr.* Changing the "Bill" to "Willie" was a playful way of using a name audiences of the 1920s would recognize, and hinted at the fun that was to follow.

Minnie makes music

Right from the start, Mickey had a romantic counterpart in Minnie Mouse. Although she was often cast in traditional female roles, there was one area in which Minnie was Mickey's equal. They both burst into song at the least excuse, and no horn sat untootled or ivories untickled when they were nearby. Mickey and Minnie never wed, but in real life, the current official voices of the characters are married.

A poster for Ye Olden Days *(1933), in which Mickey and Minnie appear in a medieval musical romance.*

A victim of the harsh effects of the Depression, Mickey nonetheless exhibits the true unselfish spirit of Christmas in Mickey's Good Deed (1932).

Color was added to Mickey's shorts (the films, not just his familiar two-button pants), in 1935's The Band Concert.

In Shanghaied *(1934), Minnie is held prisoner by Peg Leg Pete. Will Mickey be able to save her? Need one ask?*

Brave Little Tailor *showcased a redesign of Mickey and Minnie by Fred Moore. Today, many animators consider this to be Mickey and Minnie's most appealing look.*

Peg Leg Pete

The origins of the villain Mickey faced time and again can be traced back to the Alice Comedies. Peg Leg Pete (later known simply as Pete) became the Studio's favorite "heavy." He was so effective as an antagonist that he often showed up to do battle with other Studio stars, such as Donald Duck, Goofy, and Chip 'n' Dale.

Mickey comes face to face with some playful spirits in Lonesome Ghosts *(1937).*

Mickey takes on two roles in the movie The Prince and the Pauper *(1990).*

Making Mickey Move

Storyman Harry Reeves makes changes to the drawings on a storyboard for a 1930s cartoon.

MANY OF THE METHODS used by the Disney Studio in the 1930s to create animated films remain unchanged today. First, there must be a storyline—a reason for a character to be put in motion. An appropriate world for the character to inhabit must then be designed. And the animator must still create the necessary number of drawings to put a character through his paces; this can be up to 24 for each second of film time. Color must then be added to the drawings. Finally, all the various elements—drawings, backgrounds, and special camera processes—are combined with dialogue, music, and sound effects, and the film is finally complete.

Back to the storyboard

Developed at the Disney Studio, the storyboard was an efficient visual way to plan a cartoon. This procedure, in which movie scenes are carefully planned out as a series of drawings, was also used for Disney's live-action films and became standard practice for such noteworthy directors as Alfred Hitchcock and Steven Spielberg.

①

A storyboard drawing of Mickey and Pluto.

Pencil layout drawing of the train platform. The final background painting is made from this layout.

One of the many drawings for Mr. Mouse Takes a Trip (1940).

Mickey changes

Mickey has undergone numerous design changes since his creation, from his clothes to his eyes, and even his proportions. But even though some visual characteristics may have fallen by the wayside, what has remained unchanged is Mickey's bright, friendly personality and his universal appeal.

The first time Mickey was animated he had neither shoes nor gloves.

Mickey first donned gloves when he sat down at the piano in The Opry House.

By the mid-1930s, Mickey's body had become more pear-shaped and his overall look rounder and more expressive.

THE POINTER

1936

1928
PLANE CRAZY

THE OPRY HOUSE

1929
THRU THE MIRROR

By 1939 Mickey had a small eye with a pupil, instead of the large black oval eye.

1939

The finished film frames show the animation drawings inked and painted on transparent cels and placed over the final background painting.

These are just three of the many drawings required to complete the simple gesture of thumbing a ride.

②

③

Mickey lets the oncoming train know he is eager to get on board.

TR #38

Mickey's most recent theatrical short dressed him in a costume and revived body proportions inspired by his look 45 years ago.

THE SIMPLE THINGS

In the early 1940s Mickey was given two-tone, oval ears that worked in perspective.

THE LITTLE WHIRLWIND

1941

1948

By the mid-1940s Mickey's ears had resumed their rounder, all-black appearance

MICKEY DOWN UNDER

1953

In the early 1950s Mickey's appearance took on a more angular aspect.

1995

RUNAWAY BRAIN

Silly Symphonies

B Y 1929, both the movie-going public and theater owners greeted each new Mickey cartoon with enthusiasm. But Walt, along with Carl Stalling, the head of the Studio music department, wanted to try something different. They devised a series in which music would drive the action of the film and a changing cast of characters would be featured. The result was the Silly Symphonies, and the initial landmark film was *The Skeleton Dance*.

Syncopated skeletons

The Skeleton Dance featured skeletons rising from their graves and cavorting to spookily humorous melodies. It was released in August 1929 and successfully showcased animated images combined with a strong musical score.

Advancing the art of animation

The Silly Symphonies became a testing ground in which the Studio developed its storytelling skills, improved animation techniques, and introduced new technologies to the cartoon medium. A total of 75 Silly Symphonies were made between 1929 and 1939.

Flowers and Trees (1932) was the first cartoon to be filmed in three-strip Technicolor.

Babes in the Woods (1932), the story of Hansel and Gretel, was the Studio's first retelling of a European fairy tale.

THE BIG
BAD WOLF

Who's Afraid of the Big Bad Wolf?

Morale boost

1933's *Three Little Pigs* (right) is acknowledged as an early triumph in personality animation, and is one of the most famous cartoons of all time. Its success has been partly attributed to Depression-era audiences relating to the situation of having "a wolf at your door." The ability to conquer the 1930s economic crisis was symbolized by the pigs driving the wolf away.

The Goddess of Spring *(1934, left) gave Disney artists practice animating the human form.*

Songs played an essential role in advancing the storyline and defining character in *The Cookie Carnival (1935).*

Judge Owl

Jenny Wren from Who Killed Cock Robin? *(1935).*

Ready to roll

The expert personality animation of *Who Killed Cock Robin?* is said to have convinced Walt that his artists were ready to produce their first full-length animated feature.

MULTIPLANE BACKGROUND PAINTING FOR *THE OLD MILL*

New technology

The Old Mill was produced to enable the staff to gain experience using the newly developed multiplane camera. It was a painstaking process, but it gave cartoon images remarkable depth and perspective.

The multiplane camera photographed background elements that were painted on separate panes lef glass. Along with any animation cels, the positions of the panes of glass would be changed slightly for every frame of film.

Academy Awards®

THROUGHOUT MOST of the 1930s the Silly Symphonies were the sparkling jewels in the Studio's crown. Almost every Best Cartoon Academy Award® given during that period went to a Silly Symphony.

1932
FLOWERS AND TREES

The first ever Best Cartoon Academy Award® went to *Flowers and Trees.*

1933
THREE LITTLE PIGS

Everyone loved *Three Little Pigs,* including the voting members of the Academy of Motion Picture Arts and Sciences.

1935
THE TORTOISE AND THE HARE

It was no contest as *The Tortoise and the Hare* won the Best Cartoon race.

1935
THREE ORPHAN KITTENS

A convincing portrayal of the playful antics of three mischievous felines clinched the Academy Award® for *Three Orphan Kittens.*

1936
THE COUNTRY COUSIN

The centuries-old Aesop fable received a modern spin in *The Country Cousin.*

1937
THE OLD MILL

Walt Disney received a top Technical Award for the design and application of the multiplane camera, as well as an Oscar® for *The Old Mill.*

1939
THE UGLY DUCKLING

The last entry in the Silly Symphony series, *The Ugly Duckling* is also one of the Studio's most poignant films. Its Academy Award® ended the series on an appropriately high note.

Disney in Print

When the newspaper strip first appeared, it was written by Walt Disney and illustrated by Ub Iwerks.

I T WAS PERHAPS inevitable that a movie character who was made by pen and ink should make the leap to the printed page. In 1930, Mickey's antics arrived in people's homes with the debut of the Mickey Mouse newspaper strip. Both his newspaper adventures and the storybooks that followed helped to define Mickey's personality and his spirit of fun and daring. Before long, the other Disney characters followed in his literary footsteps.

Mickey Mouse Book (1930) was Mickey's first appearance in book form.

The publisher of The Adventures of Mickey Mouse Book 1 *(1931) wanted to reduce costs by printing it in black and white, but Walt insisted on color.*

Breaking into books

While newspaper publishing gave the Studio an additional source of income, both Walt and Roy wanted to provide a quality literary format for the fans of their cartoon stars. Through the years right up to the present day, major publishers in the U.S. and abroad have been licensed to produce Disney books. And in 1991, Disney set up its own publishing imprint, represented today by the Hyperion Books and Disney Editions imprints.

The Disney cartoons were so popular that this 1933 edition of Three Little Pigs *sold for $1.00, even in the midst of the tight economy of the Depression.*

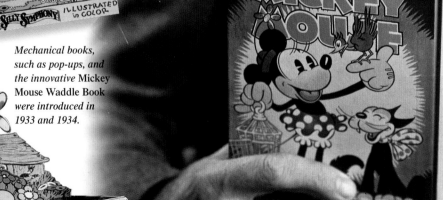

Mechanical books, such as pop-ups, and the innovative Mickey Mouse Waddle Book *were introduced in 1933 and 1934.*

Snow White *(1937) was inspired by Disney's first animated feature.*

Fantasia, *published in 1940, was the first major Disney book designed to appeal to adults. It was written by the film's narrator, Deems Taylor.*

Beautiful books

The edition of *Fantasia* pictured above was lavishly illustrated with concept and inspirational art created during the film's production. This part of the animation development process continues to fascinate, and many current books are devoted to showcasing these miniature masterpieces.

During World War II, an idea for an animated film that was never made did appear in book form. The author was RAF Flight Lieutenant Roald Dahl.

Donald Duck (1936) was the first Donald Duck book.

Licensing

Many Disney books during the 1930s were written and illustrated at the Disney Studio. But as the publishing program grew, licensed publishers assumed the role of designing many of the titles under the supervision of the Disney staff, ensuring that the quality Walt and Roy had established from the start was maintained.

Titles in the Little Golden Books series included Through the Picture Frame *(1944),* The Cold-Blooded Penguin *(1944), and* Dumbo *(1947).* Dumbo *was the first book to actually carry the LGB logo.*

Foreign editions

Today many Disney books originate with foreign publishers and are translated for the U.S. and countries around the world. And, as can be seen by this 1935 French edition of *The Grasshopper and the Ants* (below right), some books are specially designed for formats and interests within an individual country.

Little Golden Books

In 1944, Disney characters became a part of the newly introduced Little Golden Book format. The idea behind Little Golden Books was to produce small, inexpensive hardback books that everyone could afford and that children could think of as their own. The books were a huge success, and many Disney titles were produced.

Pluto

MICKEY'S FAITHFUL DOG Pluto didn't start out as Mickey's pal. In the 1930 film *The Chain Gang*, Mickey was cast in the unusual role of prison escapee and Pluto was one of the bloodhounds sent to track him down. Another detour on the way to becoming mouse's best friend occurred in Pluto's second film, *The Picnic*. He was named Rover and was Minnie's dog, not Mickey's. After that, however, the hound found the name and home he was destined to have: as Mickey's pet and best friend Pluto.

A very different-looking Pluto makes his screen debut as a bloodhound in 1930, sniffing out a prison escapee!

Pluto struggles with the good and evil sides of his nature in Lend a Paw *(1941). It won an Academy Award® for Best Cartoon.*

While delivering milk, Pluto falls for Dinah Dachshund in the 1946 short In Dutch.

In Bone Trouble *(1940), problems arise when Pluto tries to steal a bone from the dog next door!*

Mickey gives Pluto a sprucing-up in Society Dog Show *(1939).*

An early storyboard drawing of Pluto.

Silent star

Early attempts to give Pluto a voice were not successful, and it became clear that words were unnecessary for Pluto. His face was so expressive that he became one of the first cartoon characters who clearly showed reasoning and attitude solely through pantomime!

Norm Ferguson's 1934 animation of Pluto's battle with a particularly sticky strip of fly paper for Playful Pluto *was reshot in color for 1939's* The Beach Picnic. *It remains an outstanding example of the animator's art.*

Goofy

Goofy meets his match on the basketball court in Double Dribble *(1946).*

FEW CARTOON STARS have gone through as many name changes and redesigns as Goofy, while still remaining in the public's affection as being—well, Goofy. He started out as a minor character in the audience for one of Mickey's shows. His distinctive hiccupping laugh, however, ensured he was headed for stardom. He was called variously Dippy Dawg, Dippy the Goof, and in his most enduring role as one of Mickey's pals, Goofy.

Goofy first appeared in Mickey's Revue *(1932). When Mickey, Minnie, Horace, and Clarabelle put on a big show, Goofy constantly interrupts by eating peanuts and laughing, much to the annoyance of the audience.*

Goofy, as George Geef, is left holding the baby in Father's Day Off *(1953).*

In Motor Mania *(1950), cars and Goofy just don't mix.*

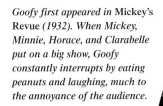

Goofy falls asleep everywhere, except when his head hits the pillow in How To Sleep *(1953).*

Goofy is bitten by the golf bug in How to Play Golf *(1944).*

Goofy's horse shows who's boss in How to Ride a Horse *(1950).*

The idea of using Goofy to demonstrate "how to" skills in a series of films obviously amused the Disney animators. Audiences found the improbable approach hilarious, too! The "lessons" began in 1941 with the How to Ride a Horse *sequence in the feature* The Reluctant Dragon *(1941).*

Goofy guy

Later, along with some design changes, Goofy was used to represent the "ordinary Joe" and was named George Geef. But for his fans who love him he will always be Goofy.

Donald Duck

Donald strikes a jaunty pose in The Wise Little Hen, *his film debut.*

It may seem surprising that one of Disney's most belligerent, unintelligible, and down-on-his-luck personalities would become one of the Studio's biggest stars, eclipsing even Mickey in popularity in less than a decade. Perhaps it was because audiences could readily identify with a character who was constantly plagued by life's frustrations but who refused to surrender without a noisy battle—good ol' Donald Duck!

Donald's incomprehensible vocalizations were spoofed by the Studio in Donald's Dream Voice. *A pill makes him speak like a sophisticated leading man.*

Donald proves his ability to get into the swing of things during the gang's vacation in Hawaiian Holiday *(1937).*

One popular duck

Donald made his screen debut in *The Wise Little Hen*, a Silly Symphony from 1934. His costar in that film, Peter Pig, quickly faded from the scene, but Donald was a duck who refused to go quietly. He was quickly added to Mickey's growing group of friends, appearing as a sidekick and troublemaker in many of Mickey's films throughout the 1930s. Donald also had his own series of cartoons by the late 1930s, eventually starring in 128 cartoons—more than any other Disney headliner!

Even though his first appearance was in color, Donald's early roles in the Mickey shorts were in glorious black and white.

Daisy

Adding to Donald's happiness and vexation is his heartthrob Daisy. She can be charming and sweet—and as hot-tempered as her volatile boyfriend when she doesn't get her own way.

The nephews

Donald's trio of nephews, Huey, Dewey, and Louie, have continued to plague their exasperated uncle from their screen debut in 1938 to the present day.

Donald opens the door to a triumvirate of trouble in these storyboard drawings for the cartoon Donald's Nephews *(1938).*

SCENE FROM
SOUP'S ON (1948)

In Canvas Back Duck *(1953), Donald discovers his oversized boxing opponent Pete has a glass jaw! (right)*

CHIP 'N' DALE

Donald contends with Spike the Bee.

Donald meets his nemeses

It seems everywhere Donald turned he had a battle on his hands. Whether he faced a massive menace, like Pete, or mischievous chipmunks, like Chip 'n' Dale, Donald almost always met his match. In fact, the smaller his opponent, the greater Donald's downfall.

With costars Chip 'n' Dale, and Dolores the elephant, in Working for Peanuts *(1953).*

Donald tried his hand at a wide variety of jobs in his films—with little success!

A little education

Donald starred in several films that dealt with educational subjects in a humorous but informative way. The most popular was *Donald in Mathmagic Land* in which the famous duck discovers the importance arithmetical principles play in every aspect of people's lives.

The factory nurse tends to an injury-prone Donald in How to Have an Accident at Work *(1959).*

DONALD IN MATHMAGIC LAND (1959)

Donald and the Wheel

Donald and the Wheel cast the puzzled duck as the anonymous caveman inventor of the wheel. Overwhelmed by the wheel's far-ranging uses, Donald eventually refuses to take responsibility for it. He exits the film pulling a sled in a vain attempt to get away from his invention altogether!

Right from the start Donald was a popular merchandise personality, as seen in this 1930s bisque figurine (right).

DONALD AND
THE WHEEL (1961)

21

Merchandise

WOODEN MICKEY FIGURE

1930

1935

1947

MICKEY MOUSE was the first cartoon character to be extensively merchandised. Hundreds of Mickey items were produced during the 1930s, the height of the Great Depression, creating jobs for many people during a time of need. Along with Mickey, other Disney stars began appearing on everything from clothing to toys. Disney characters didn't just appeal to children, and eventually products began to be specially designed with adults in mind. Today, Disney merchandise is treasured by young and old alike as a way of sharing in the adventures and fun of the Studio's family of stars, of reliving childhood memories, and of appreciating the superb artistry behind the graphic design of animation.

Here comes Donald Duck!

Not long after his movie debut in *The Wise Little Hen* (1934), Donald Duck joined Mickey and Minnie as a highly popular merchandise item. Here he is pictured as a stuffed doll from the mid-1930s (left) and (above) paired with Goofy, his frequent costar, on a tin windup action toy manufactured by Louis Marx & Co. in 1947.

MICKEY AND MINNIE HANDCAR

1934

Mickey's magic

The first licensed Disney toy was a wooden figure of Mickey Mouse. It was manufactured in 1930 by George Borgfeld & Co. of New York and designed by Disney artist Bert Gillett. Proof of Mickey's merchandising magic was soon clear for all to see. In 1934, the Lionel Corporation had been in receivership with liabilities amounting to $296,000. Shortly after producing the Mickey and Minnie handcar shown above, the firm reported assets of $2,000,000!

1930s

Imported from Japan, these figurines came in many different sizes and poses.

MINNIE AND MICKEY BISQUE FIGURINES

Mouse with dewdrop, from Bambi

Classic collection

Plane Crazy Mickey

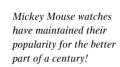

The Walt Disney Classics Collection began in 1992. The aim was to introduce a fine line of highly collectible porcelain sculptures that were each inspired by delightful moments from the animated movies. For the first time not only were the carefully sculpted figurines closely based on animation drawings, but the actual original film colors were also carefully researched and duplicated—resulting in the most authentic Disney figurines ever manufactured.

It's for you!

In the mid-1970s the American Telephone Corporation chose Mickey Mouse to be the star of their first-ever character telephone.

MICKEY MOUSE TELEPHONE

1970s

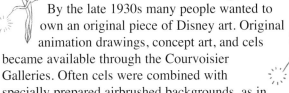

Perfect timing

During the Great Depression of the 1930s, when many companies were forced to lay off workers and close their doors, the Ingersoll-Waterbury Clock Company was in the happy position of having to add 2,700 employees to its staff of 300— all thanks to the success of the Mickey Mouse watches it had started manufacturing.

POCKET WATCH

Mickey Mouse watches have maintained their popularity for the better part of a century!

1930s

1930s

WRISTWATCH

This wooden Minnie Mouse figure has a cloth plaid skirt.

1950s

MICKEY MOUSE PHONOGRAPH

Hi kids!

Original artwork

By the late 1930s many people wanted to own an original piece of Disney art. Original animation drawings, concept art, and cels became available through the Courvoisier Galleries. Often cels were combined with specially prepared airbrushed backgrounds, as in this example of the mushroom dancers from *Fantasia*.

Musical mouse

The Disney toy designers have always looked for fun ways to make the characters part of the product. For this record player from the 1950s, Mickey's hand serves as the phonograph arm, making him a vital part of the machine's music-making.

Snow White and the Seven Dwarfs

Acknowledging the story's literary roots, the film opens with an elaborately illuminated storybook.

THE HOLLYWOOD community dubbed Walt's attempt to create the first feature-length animated cartoon as "Disney's Folly." But Walt and his staff fully believed in their plans for the groundbreaking *Snow White and the Seven Dwarfs*. When the film premiered in December 1937, all the hard work, attention to detail, and inspiration paid off. *Snow White* was a critical success and became the highest-grossing film to date.

"One Song" is the Prince's declaration of his love for Snow White.

The Snow White operetta

The Studio realized the importance music played in storytelling while working on the *Silly Symphonies*. *Snow White* was developed almost like an operetta. Musical themes underscore almost all of the action, and the songs are seamlessly woven into the storyline, furthering plot and enhancing characterization.

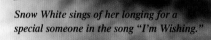

Snow White sings of her longing for a special someone in the song "I'm Wishing."

THE WICKED QUEEN

In order to escape the Queen, Snow White seeks refuge in the cottage of the Seven Dwarfs.

Color palette

Snow White was released at a time when virtually every feature film was in black and white. Since critics feared audiences couldn't tolerate the bright colors associated with animated cartoons for the length of a feature, the color palette for *Snow White* was given careful consideration.

The Dwarfs' costumes stressed earth tones and muted colors, rather than the bright colors normally used for comic personalities.

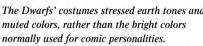

Snow White's connection to the Dwarfs is established even before she meets them, when she cleans their cottage to the tune "Whistle While You Work."

The Dwarfs reveal both their occupation and work ethic with the cheery "Heigh-Ho."

The Queen's jealousy of Snow White is so intense that she sheds her prized beauty in order to assume the guise of a haggard old crone.

Their willingness to please Snow White is demonstrated when the Dwarfs step up to the washtub with a "Bluddle-Uddle-Um-Dum."

Fairy-tale world

The film's restrained color palette was not just a concession to fears. It captured the old-world timelessness of the story and became an essential ingredient in bringing a fairy-tale world to life.

Reflecting Snow White's lifted spirits, "The Silly Song" sets the stage for festivities at the cottage.

During the movie's conclusion the Prince's "One Song" and Snow White's "Some Day My Prince Will Come" are reprised for one of filmdom's most exuberantly happy finales.

At the Dwarfs' request Snow White shares her dream in "Some Day My Prince Will Come."

Moving up

With the profits from *Snow White*, land was purchased in Burbank, California, and a new facility was constructed specifically designed for the needs of animation.

Walt with the Seven Dwarfs on the cover of Time *magazine.*

TIME
The Weekly Newsmagazine

BANCROFT PUBLIC LIBRARY
6355 S. 77th St.
alston, NE 68127

Fantasy Worlds

THE 1930s CONCLUDED with the outstanding success of *Snow White and the Seven Dwarfs*. An ambitious program of animated features immediately began, but the outbreak of World War II caused a sharp economic downturn for the Studio and, as the 1940s ended, its future seemed in doubt.

Pinocchio

IN ADAPTING Carlo Collodi's tale of Pinocchio, a wooden puppet who longs to become a real boy, the Disney storytellers created a delightful and convincing storybook world. The movie is filled with sumptuous artwork, unforgettable characters, and wonderful songs—as well as some very dark and sinister scenes! Surprisingly, the film was not as successful on release as first hoped, but years later it took its rightful place among Disney's most beloved classics.

Animators studied three-dimensional models to make the film.

Audiences delighted in the fanciful clocks and toys in Geppetto's workshop. These clocks were the imaginative designs of Albert Hurter.

Attention to detail

Pinocchio's two concept artists, Gustav Tenggren and Albert Hurter, brought unique artistic imagination to their work. Audiences felt they were really walking the streets of Pinocchio's quaint Alpine village and visiting Geppetto's workshop (right).

THE BLUE FAIRY

The enchanting Blue Fairy from the Wishing Star brings Pinocchio to life.

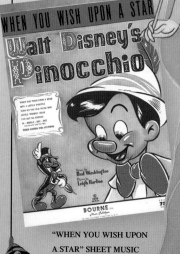

"WHEN YOU WISH UPON A STAR" SHEET MUSIC

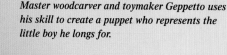

Master woodcarver and toymaker Geppetto uses his skill to create a puppet who represents the little boy he longs for.

When you wish...

Sung by Jiminy Cricket, the movie's Oscar®-winning theme song "When You Wish Upon a Star" became a statement of hope at a time when the world was in the throes of war. Other memorable songs from the movie include, "I've Got No Strings," "Give a Little Whistle," and "Hi-Diddle-Dee-Dee."

Jiminy Cricket guides the audience through the episodic story. He is Pinocchio's conscience, and the first of many small companions in Disney features who befriend and help the hero.

Gustav Tenggren created many watercolor concept paintings for the movie, and his skill at storytelling through illustration had a great influence on the film's final look.

Magical moments

One of the joys of animation is the audience's acceptance of the illogical. Jiminy has had no trouble breathing while walking along the seabed. But when he's trapped inside an air bubble that starts filling with water, he struggles as if drowning. When the bubble bursts, he is once again okay. Implausible, but the gag worked!

Pinocchio is an innocent in a world where temptations lurk around every corner.

By saving his father from Monstro, Pinocchio proves himself brave, truthful, and unselfish, and worthy of becoming the real boy Geppetto wished for.

Villains gallery

Pinocchio has to face four very different types of Disney villains: the ruthless showman, Stromboli; the tricksters Honest John and his partner Gideon; the evil Coachman; and the terrifying Monstro the Whale.

Stromboli

One of the most villainous members in the Disney gallery of infamy is the bombastic puppet master, Stromboli. He makes no secret of his plan to do away with Pinocchio after the puppet has outlived his usefulness.

Honest John and Gideon lure the gullible little puppet away from his schoolwork for a life in show business... and for their own selfish gains!

THE COACHMAN AND HIS REPENTANT VICTIMS

HONEST JOHN AND GIDEON

The Coachman

The demonic Coachman's bright red coat and jolly face disguise his ruthless determination to lead foolish boys to "Pleasure Island" and turn them into donkeys. He then plans to sell the donkeys into slavery in the salt mines.

Fantasia

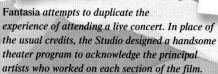

WALT DISNEY OFTEN claimed his entertainment empire "was all started by a mouse." The same could be said for one of the most ambitious and unique movies in the history of the Studio. The original plan was to make a standard Mickey Mouse short set to the music of Dukas's "The Sorcerer's Apprentice," and a famed conductor was invited to participate. But as work progressed, Walt and his staff became increasingly excited about the possibilities of combining classical music and elaborate, visual storytelling in ways that hadn't been attempted before. The final result was *Fantasia* (1940).

Fantasia attempts to duplicate the experience of attending a live concert. In place of the usual credits, the Studio designed a handsome theater program to acknowledge the principal artists who worked on each section of the film.

Toccata and Fugue in D Minor

Fantasia opens with an overture that tells no story but paints across the motion-picture screen colors and moving forms inspired by Johann Sebastian Bach's magnificent *Toccata and Fugue in D Minor*.

The Nutcracker Suite

The shimmering beauty and exquisite detail created by Disney special effects in *The Nutcracker Suite* remain unsurpassed even today. They superbly capture the delicate, intimate world of plants and woodland fairies.

Mickey's role as an apprentice sorcerer (below) is his greatest performance—despite the fact that there is not a line of dialogue or narration during the entire sequence!

The Sorcerer's Apprentice

The Sorcerer's Apprentice tells the tale of a wizard's apprentice who tries to use magic to fill his master's water vat—with chaotic results! The above image shows concept art of magic out of control, as an army of enchanted brooms fills a cavernous room with buckets of water.

The Rite of Spring

Stravinsky's powerful score serves as a musical background for Earth's turbulent evolution, from its explosive creation to the era of the dinosaurs and their eventual extinction.

The Pastoral Symphony

Beethoven's musical setting for a day in the country was combined with an entrancing glimpse of Mt. Olympus, home of the Greek gods and of mythological creatures such as fauns, centaurs, unicorns, and flying horses.

Bill Tytla's animation of the demon Chernabog in Night on Bald Mountain *is still acclaimed for its raw power and embodiment of consuming evil. The entire sequence of the wild revelry of lost souls and monstrous apparitions is regarded as the Studio's consummate depiction of evil.*

Concept art of a virile centaur.

A model of "prima ballerina" Hyacinth Hippo.

Dance of the Hours

Pirouetting hippos and agile alligators were hilarious choices as members of a *corps de ballet* in *Dance of the Hours*, but the animators took care to blend the characters' comic performances with correct dance movements.

Animators studied ballet performances to ensure that the dance sequences were realistic.

A poster from Fantasia's original release in 1940 (left).

Night on Bald Mountain

Night on Bald Mountain flows seamlessly into *Ave Maria*, symbolizing the triumph of good over evil, the light of the faithful defeating the powers of darkness. *Ave Maria* is the only sequence in *Fantasia* to add a chorus and solo voice to the orchestral presentation.

Dumbo

Dumbo's heartwarming appeal is captured in this recent Members Only sculpture from the Walt Disney Collectors Society.

Dumbo eventually becomes the star of the circus—using his enormous ears to fly!

DUMBO IS THE simple story of a baby elephant who overcomes the handicap of oversized ears to become the star of the circus. Unlike the elaborate features *Pinocchio* and *Fantasia*, this appealing tale traveled through production relatively smoothly and within a modest budget. Both critics and the public took the story to their hearts, and Dumbo (1941) became the Studio's first profitable animated feature since Snow White and the Seven Dwarfs.

Little circus train

Casey Jr. is the little circus train with a personality! Before *Dumbo* was released, Casey Jr. appeared in *The Reluctant Dragon*, helping to demonstrate the Studio's creative use of sound effects in films. In the 1950s, he began carrying visitors on regular excursions through the enchanted realms of *Storybook Land* in Disneyland Park.

Timothy is the brash circus mouse who befriends Dumbo and pushes the elephant toward his eventual triumph.

TIMOTHY Q. MOUSE

The train arrives at its destination at night during a heavy rainstorm.

Dumbo *opens at night with storks delivering new babies to the circus.*

Morning breaks bathed in sunshine as performers and animals depart on Casey Jr., the circus train.

Bright colors

A concern then existed that prolonged exposure to bright colors might make movie audiences ill. But the film was set in the world of the circus, and vibrant colors were an essential part of capturing the atmosphere of the Big Top. The solution was to alternate bright sequences with darker ones, giving the audience a chance to recover!

Bambi

BASED ON Felix Salten's novel, *Bambi* tells the story of a young deer growing up in the forest with his friends Thumper the rabbit and Flower the skunk. The tale was different from anything the Studio had attempted before in that it featured tragic and frightening scenes such as the killing of Bambi's mother by hunters and a forest fire. However, this charming film has endured and still delights audiences today.

Studies were made of animal locomotion so that movement could be portrayed convincingly.

Baby animals

Bambi was originally planned to be the Studio's second animated feature. But the degree of realism Walt wanted for Bambi and his forest friends required a great deal of study and training on the part of his animators. This process could not be rushed if the film were to scale the artistic heights that Walt had envisioned. At last, in 1942, *Bambi* had its premiere.

Early character designs for the young fawn show the realistic approach to animal anatomy that was required for Bambi.

Bambi tries to resist the irresistible call of springtime romance, which Friend Owl calls becoming "twitterpated."

Bambi and Faline celebrate their love for each other.

Circle of life

Bambi's underlying theme—how nature renews itself as season follows season—would be repeated when Disney photographers ventured into the wilds to film real animals for the *True-Life Adventure* series. And it would provide the opening theme for the most successful animated film of all time, when audiences thrilled to the gathering of animals set to "The Circle of Life" in *The Lion King*.

An early sketch of Flower the skunk. Bambi first meets him in a bed of flowers, hence his name!

The young Prince of the Forest encounters the wonders of his woodland home.

"Look, the water's stiff," proclaims Thumper, as he introduces Bambi to the fun of skating on a frozen pond!

The War Years

I N THE EARLY 1940s, Walt Disney was asked to tour South America as a goodwill ambassador. He undertook the trip accompanied by several artists and musicians, to gather material for some animated films about the region, as well as to meet with artists and officials in the various countries. The two films that resulted were fantastically successful and helped to cement good relations between the U.S. and South America at a time when World War II was casting a shadow over the world. Animation had grown up and proved itself to be a powerful force in the cause of democracy!

"Llama Serenade" (above) was based on an ancient Inca melody.

Saludos!

The first film to result from the South American trip was *Saludos Amigos*, which featured Goofy as an Argentine gaucho (left) and Donald Duck as a tourist in Peru (right).

Donald is captivated by Brazilian artiste Aurora Miranda (right).

Mary Blair

Mary Blair was one of the artists who accompanied Walt to South America to gather inspiration for the proposed animated films. Her beautiful watercolors had a great influence on the look of the final films.

Combining live-action performers with the cartoon antics of Donald and pals in The Three Caballeros was made possible by new film processes created by technical wizard Ub Iwerks, Mickey's first animator.

The Mickey and Donald newspaper comic strips reflected life on the wartime home front.

Building morale

The Studio answered hundreds of requests from servicemen for Disney-designed insignia for their units. The Studio provided these free of charge, for as Walt explained, "How could you turn them down? They meant a lot to the men who were fighting." Many servicemen could identify with Donald cartoons such as *Fall Out—Fall In*, in which the unlucky duck endured all the rigors and trials of an army inductee, including every recruit's first foe—the drill sergeant!

The Disney artists and musicians admired the Latin American music from the regions they visited. English lyrics were added to many songs by South American composers.

Fall Out—Fall In poster (1943), featuring a military Donald Duck!

"The Yankee Doodle Spirit" was featured in the Donald Duck film The New Spirit (1942), which was designed to show how vital it was to the war effort for people to pay their income tax.

A dog's contribution

Pluto also did his bit in the military. His film *Canine Patrol*, was dedicated to the many dogs that served the U.S. Coast Guard as guardians of the country's shoreline.

Pluto lends a paw in Private Pluto *(1943), directed by Clyde Geronimi.*

In Victory Vehicles *(1943), Goofy demonstrates a number of wacky ways folks could overcome the chronic gasoline and rubber shortages of wartime.*

Mirror images

Animator Ward Kimball brings Panchito the Mexican charro rooster to life. Kimball's career at Disney spanned five decades, and included directing the Academy Award®-winning short *It's Tough to Be a Bird* (1969).

The World of Disney Comics

THE GLOBAL SUCCESS of the Disney characters has been sustained and enhanced by the many artists and writers who have created funny and exciting stories for comic books. Disney comic art was started by American artists such as Ub Iwerks, Floyd Gottfredson, and Al Taliaferro. And as both author and artist, Carl Barks set a standard that continues to be emulated and maintained by Disney comic book artists around the world.

International storytellers

Today, Disney comic books have virtually disappeared from the U.S. marketplace, but in Europe and elsewhere they continue to be an important part of the culture. In fact, the popularity of comics outside of the United States has resulted in many international artists rising to the forefront of Disney storytelling.

Although reprinted newspaper comic strips had been featured in the Mickey Mouse Magazine *of the 1930s, the first true monthly Disney comic book in the U.S. was* Walt Disney's Comics and Stories.

Barks created Disney's most popular comic book character when he introduced Donald's miserly uncle Scrooge McDuck, supposedly the world's richest man, in a 1948 story.

The King of Comics

Carl Barks worked at the Disney Studio briefly, first as an animator and then as a story artist for several Donald Duck cartoons. In the comics, he would transform the Duck clan into articulate, humorous, and spirited individuals and launch them on many a memorable adventure. Barks began his comic book career with *Donald Duck Finds Pirate Gold*, which he adapted with Jack Hannah from a proposed theatrical cartoon.

Former animator Paul Murry's depiction of Mickey Mouse in comic books (left) achieved universal popularity and was often imitated.

Giovan Battista Carpi working at his drawing board.

Disney draftsmen

Bringing their own unique approach and excellent draftsmanship to the Disney comics created in Italy, artists such as Romano Scarpa, Giovan Battista Carpi, and Giorgio Cavazanno have earned high marks from Disney fans around the world.

Many outstanding artists and writers have contributed to Topolino, an Italian publication begun in the early 1930s that is still extremely popular today.

Disney Babies (above), having fun at Christmastime, as drawn by Marin.

Disney ducks and babies

France's Claude Marin has been especially adept at capturing the world of the Disney Babies. In Scandinavia, where Donald and his relatives are hugely popular, many fine artists, such as Vicar, have contributed to the Duck legacy begun by Barks.

The Postwar Years

The first package feature to be released was Make Mine Music *in 1946. It comprised 10 individual sequences.*

IN ORDER TO resume normal feature production after the war, the Studio relied on "package pictures"—groups of short cartoons sent out together as a feature. These features were less expensive and quicker to produce, as they did not need the years of pre-planning and animation of a single story film. Walt also began filming live-action stories, which were combined with cartoon sequences. However, owing to these films' limited success, Walt knew they would have to take a gamble and return to full-length animated feature production—or close their doors for good!

Peter and the Wolf

Peter and the Wolf was originally developed as a replacement sequence for *Fantasia*. But when those plans were abandoned it was included in *Make Mine Music*. A droll narration by Sterling Holloway was added to Prokofiev's musical children's tale.

IVAN

SASHA

PETER

SONIA

BRER BEAR

Song of the South *featured the adventures of Brer Rabbit, Brer Fox, and Brer Bear.*

BRER RABBIT

JAMES BASKETT RECEIVES HIS ACADEMY AWARD®

For Song of the South, *Walt Disney sent concept artist Mary Blair to Georgia to research settings for the film's backgrounds (above).*

1946

BRER FOX

An Oscar® winner

Song of the South (1946) combined a live-action storyline with three animated sequences based on the classic Brer Rabbit tales by Joel Chandler Harris. These cartoon sequences are still highly regarded for their entertaining character animation. For his heartwarming portrayal of legendary storyteller Uncle Remus, James Baskett was presented with a special Academy Award®, making him the first-ever black male actor to receive an Oscar®.

Mickey and the Beanstalk

Before the war, an adaptation of the Jack and the Beanstalk tale had been planned as the first Mickey Mouse feature. Its years of development can be traced by the changes in Mickey's design from various storyboards. The story would finally be used as one of the sequences in *Fun and Fancy Free* (1947).

Storyboard art showing two-tone ears (early 1940s) and solid black eyes (late 1930s).

The character art for Once Upon a Wintertime *in* Melody Time *was more stylized than in any other Disney film up to that date.*

1948

1948

A frantic bee flies through a surreal world where music motifs have gone wild in Bumble Boogie.

Colorful folklore

Package features offered the opportunity for visual experimentation in color and design and provided Disney with its first excursions into American folklore, as seen in the tales of Johnny Appleseed and Pecos Bill and the adaptation of Washington Irving's *The Legend of Sleepy Hollow*.

1949

The appearance of the Headless Horseman in The Adventures of Ichabod and Mr. Toad *(1949) heralds the start of one of the most terrifying and hilarious chases ever animated.*

Walt felt a strong connection to the story for 1949's So Dear to My Heart (above and right). It was a way for Walt to put on film the way of life he fondly remembered from his childhood in Marceline, Missouri.

CONCEPT ART BY C. GILLINGWATER

39

Moving On

AFTER THE WAR, Walt continued with many new and diverse projects, but undoubtedly the boldest venture of the 1950s was his decision to build a theme park that would be unlike any other the public had experienced. He named it Disneyland.

Cinderella

Cinderella's snooty stepsisters, Anastasia and Drizella, flounce off to the ball with high expectations.

Eleanor Audley poses for the character of the wicked stepmother.

THE CINDERELLA STORY IS one of the world's oldest fairy tales: different versions appear throughout the world, from Asia to the Native American cultures. When the Disney writers approached this beloved story, they kept its timeless themes: a young girl dressed in rags and forced to be a servant by her envious stepmother; a ball; a charming prince; a helpful fairy godmother. Then they added a houseful of mice, birds, and other animals, whose entertaining antics are cleverly woven into the storyline. The result is truly magical.

A story sketch from 1933 shows Cinderella helping one of her stepsisters.

The Stepmother

Animator Frank Thomas, who helped bring the stepmother to life, commented that she was one of the most realistic characters he had ever done. Her elegant, subtle villainy owed a great deal to Eleanor Audley, the actress who provided the character's voice and performed as her model.

A transformation

The Studio had considered making a Silly Symphony of *Cinderella* as far back as 1933, when it developed a rough outline and some story sketches. Seventeen years later, like the transformation of Cinderella's rags into a beautiful gown, these early attempts were embellished and turned into a story filled with humor, romance, and appealing characters.

Actress Helene Stanley, seen here with sequence director Wilfred Jackson, took the role of Cinderella as reference for the animators.

Mary Blair worked as a Disney concept artist for animated and live-action films between 1939 and 1953. Walt admired her whimsical design sense and imaginative use of color.

Concept art of Cinderella at work.

Makeover magic

"Let's see, dear…your size…and the shade of your eyes…ah… something simple—but daring, too. Just leave it to me. What a gown this will be," says the Fairy Godmother. And with a wave of her wand, Cinderella is ready for the ball.

Costume designs for Cinderella and Prince Charming by Mary Blair depict an earlier historic setting than was chosen for the final film.

Magical mice

During an early story conference Walt commented that the idea of having the mice wear clothes might be fun. He also thought that the audience might find the character of Cinderella more endearing if they saw her brightening her drab days by making clothes for her little friends.

Concept art of the mice by story artist Bill Peet…

…and how Gus and Jaq and some of their friends appear in the final film.

Timeless music

Cinderella was the first traditional feature for which Walt went outside the Studio's own songwriting teams for a full score of songs. Al Hoffman, Mack David, and Jerry Livingston produced a truly captivating score.

Cinderella finds romance with a handsome stranger at the ball (above).

Ilene Woods (right) made a demo recording for "A Dream Is a Wish Your Heart Makes." Walt was so impressed by her performance, he asked her to provide Cinderella's speaking and singing voice.

The Cinderella songs were the first sheet music released by the Walt Disney Music Company.

43

Live-Action Movies

ALTHOUGH A FEW live-action Disney movies, such as *So Dear to My Heart*, were made at the Studio in the 1940s, they had still relied on animation sequences to enhance their appeal. *Treasure Island*, made in England and released in 1950, was the first Disney feature without any animation at all. It was followed by several other British productions and by the mid-1950s, Walt was ready to begin a regular live-action program at home, starting with *20,000 Leagues Under the Sea*.

The battle with a giant squid—storyboard art and the movie scene.

Discovering treasure

Treasure Island was Disney's first all live-action feature. Released in 1950, it generated some of the best reviews Disney had received in almost a decade. In the movie, Robert Newton gave a memorable performance as Robert Louis Stevenson's lovable rogue Long John Silver.

Treasure Island was an important film for Disney, and Walt traveled to England to see the production for himself.

Deep sea drama

Produced at Disney's Burbank Studio, *20,000 Leagues Under the Sea*, based on the classic novel by Jules Verne, received all the attention and high production values associated with the animated films. It also featured a high-powered performance by James Mason as Captain Nemo, the anguished commander of the submarine *Nautilus*.

THE MIGHTIEST MOTION PICTURE OF THEM ALL!

Walt Disney

20,000 Leagues UNDER THE Sea

Starring

KIRK DOUGLAS · JAMES MASON
PAUL LUKAS · PETER LORRE

TECHNICOLOR

CINEMASCOPE

The poster for 20,000 Leagues Under the Sea (1954) *captures the excitement and mystery of the film.*

ROBERT NEWTON
WITH BOBBY
DRISCOLL AS JIM
HAWKINS (RIGHT)

The court of King Henry VIII was the setting for dashing swordplay, romance, and despicable villainy when Charles Major's novel "When Knighthood Was in Flower" was filmed as The Sword and the Rose (1953).

20,000 Leagues Under the Sea *won an Academy Award® for Art Direction and Set Decoration. And Nemo's spectacular organ eventually found a home in the* Haunted Mansion *at Disneyland.*

Family features

The Studio's live-action film program was specially designed to appeal to a family audience. In addition to adventures like *20,000 Leagues Under the Sea*, it included historical dramas, animal stories, fantasies, special-effects comedies, literary favorites, classic family adventures, and musicals.

Old Yeller *(1957) tells the story of a brave mongrel dog who befriends two boys on a ranch in Texas in the 1860s.*

Who wouldn't believe in leprechauns when the Disney effects wizards portrayed their existence so convincingly in 1959's Darby O'Gill and the Little People*!*

Pollyanna is awed by the magnificence of her wealthy aunt's home in this concept art for the 1960 movie adaptation of Eleanor H. Porter's popular novel.

THE GREATEST ADVENTURE STORY OF THEM ALL!

WALT DISNEY'S
SWISS FAMILY ROBINSON

TECHNICOLOR
FILMED IN PANAVISION

JOHN MILLS DOROTHY McGUIRE JAMES MacARTHUR JANET MUNRO
SESSUE HAYAKAWA TOMMY KIRK KEVIN CORCORAN CECIL PARKER ANDY HO MILTON REID LARRI TAYLOR

Desert island adventure

Swiss Family Robinson (1960) was one of Disney's most successful live-action movies ever. It tells of a family who survives a shipwreck and is washed up on a tropical island. The Robinsons ingeniously build a wonderful tree house from the wreck, forage for food and even fight off a band of pirates. Packed with excitement, adventure, and romance, the movie has something for everyone.

Swiss Family Robinson *was such a hit it was released five times in theaters before coming out on video in 1982.*

Costume design for Gonzorgo, from Babes in Toyland.

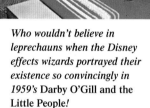

Costume design for Babes in Toyland *character Mary Contrary.*

Babes in Toyland

Babes in Toyland was originally made in 1935 starring comedy duo Laurel and Hardy. Walt had allowed the song "Who's Afraid of the Big Bad Wolf" to be used in a scene featuring the Three Little Pigs. In 1961, Walt remade the movie himself—his first live-action musical.

Alice in Wonderland

ALICE TUMBLED INTO her dream Wonderland. The Disney Studio's own journey into Lewis Carroll's bizarre world was not nearly so rapid! Throughout the 1930s and into the 1940s, scripts were developed, a psychoanalyst was brought in to provide insights into the story, and even the input of Aldous Huxley, the famous British novelist, was sought. But Walt was still not satisfied, and it was unclear whether *Alice* would be a full, live-action feature, or part cartoon. By the late 1940s the decision was finally made to create an all-animated production.

Fanciful paintings
Color and styling for the final film was inspired by the fanciful paintings of Mary Blair, including the Mad Hatter's tea party (above) and the Queen of Hearts' castle (right).

Verse!

will you walk a lit-tle faster said a whiting to a snail, there's a por-poise close be-hind us and he's tread-ing on my

Various composers wrote more than 40 songs for the film during its years of development. However, only 15 of these were heard in the final film. Above is a portion of an unused song, with music by Frank Churchill set to Lewis Carroll's original lyrics.

Story reels
By the late 1930s a version of the entire film, using the delightful drawings of illustrator David Hall, was put onto story reels with a temporary (called "scratch" in the film industry) soundtrack.

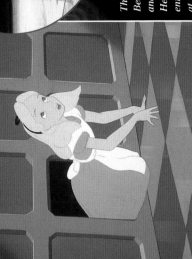

The young actress Kathryn Beaumont provided Alice's voice and visual reference for the film. Here she models for Alice's entrance into the room she finds at the bottom of the rabbit hole

THE MAD HATTER

THE MARCH HARE

Land of wonder

Alice in Wonderland may be among the public's least favorite of the animated features produced by Walt, but it is admired by Disney fans for its imaginative design work and the lively animation of its cast of unique and humorous characters.

THE GRINNING
CHESHIRE CAT

No heart

Alice's charming and highly regarded story caused Walt some problems—especially bringing some of the bizarre adventures to the big screen. Walt didn't feel that it worked well and later commented that his *Alice* had no "heart."

The Queen of Hearts represented an abusive absolute monarchy, in which "all ways are my ways."

Talking flowers

Many of the film's character designs were influenced by the original Sir John Tenniel book illustrations. But the Disney artists utilized their own formidable artistic imaginations to portray the very humanlike residents of the garden of live flowers.

Nana, the nursemaid dog.

Peter Pan

MICHAEL

TINKER BELL

CAPTAIN HOOK

ALIVE WITH pirates, Indians, mermaids, an impish fairy, and a boy who could fly, *Peter Pan* was ideally suited for the Disney storytellers and was moved into development in the late 1930s following the success of *Snow White*. By the early 1940s a great deal of progress had been made, but wartime grounded *Peter Pan*, and it would not be ready to fly into theaters until 1953.

First designs

These rough designs from 1940 are clearly recognizable as the personalities who would appear on the screen more than a decade later, from Michael Darling and his ever-present teddy bear, to the foppish Captain Hook, and the sprightly Tinker Bell.

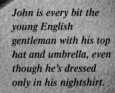

John is every bit the young English gentleman with his top hat and umbrella, even though he's dressed only in his nightshirt.

Michael is carried aloft thanks to his youthful trust—and a generous helping of pixie dust.

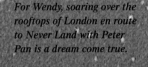

For Wendy, soaring over the rooftops of London en route to Never Land with Peter Pan is a dream come true.

The original concept

As he had done for *Alice in Wonderland*, David Hall provided lively inspirational art for *Peter Pan*, capturing all the magic and wonder experienced by Wendy and her brothers as they set out for their joyous adventure with Peter Pan in Never Land.

Tinker Bell's jealous nature was displayed even before Wendy left the nursery (above).

An early sketch of Tinker Bell sitting on an alphabet block.

Light fairy

The Disney film breaks with the stage tradition of having Tinker Bell represented by a dancing spotlight. Through the magic of animation, Tinker Bell became a fully visualized character.

MARY BLAIR ART

Fantasy art

Mary Blair contributed concept art for the movie. Whether dark and mysterious or playful and sprightly, her paintings captured the fantasy of Never Land perfectly and had a great influence on the style and look of the final movie. *Peter Pan* has proved to be a timeless favorite and was re-released in theaters five times before coming out on video in 1990.

Pan holds an injured Tinker Bell whose light is fading.

The menacing presence of Captain Hook.

Peter Pan is the boy who never grew up. He is the spirit of youth, a joy forgotten by many an adult.

Colorful buccaneers aboard Hook's pirate ship, The Jolly Roger.

Lost boys

The Disney artists chose to dress Peter's "men," the Lost Boys, in animal fur, and changed their names from the Barrie originals, such as the Twins, Tootles, Nibs, Slightly, and Curly to the Raccoon Twins, Cubby, and Foxy.

Hans Conried plays a mean and moody Captain Hook.

Quite a perfomance

Disney honored the *Peter Pan* stage tradition of having the same actor portray both Mr. Darling and Captain Hook by casting Hans Conried as the voice for both characters. Conried also provided visual inspiration for the animators through virtuoso performances of the roles during reference filming.

Hook's archenemy is the tick-tocking Crocodile, who bit off his hand years before—hence the hook!

The Musical World of Disney

ZIP-A-DEE-DOO-DAH. HEIGH-HO. Hakuna Matata. Bibbidi-Bobbidi-Boo! Disney music is full of fun and magic, as well as expressions of hope, such as "A Dream Is a Wish Your Heart Makes" and "When You Wish Upon a Star." All of these wonderful songs have something in common: they were composed as important parts of the *story*. There is no doubt that everyone involved in the Disney musical legacy over the years has helped to create some of the most memorable music ever to come out of Hollywood!

"Minnie's Yoo Hoo" was the first original song composed for a Disney film; it was published in 1930, making it the first piece of Disney sheet music.

A segment of Make Mine Music *(1946) was about the romance between a boy and a girl hat. It was sung by the famous trio The Andrews Sisters.*

Songs were written for live-action dramatic storylines, too.

Disney's first big song success was "Who's Afraid of the Big Bad Wolf." It has been recorded many times, and translated into many languages—truly a worldwide hit!

The first major publisher of Disney sheet music was Irving Berlin, Inc.

The songwriting team of Frank Churchill and Larry Morey wrote a memorable score for Disney's first feature, Snow White and the Seven Dwarfs. *They then created songs for* Bambi *and began working on* The Wind in the Willows *and* Peter Pan.

"I'm Wishing" was the first of eight Churchill/Morey songs sung in Snow White.

The emphasis on musical numbers in the 1940s package features made songs from productions such as Make Mine Music *and* Fun and Fancy Free *a natural for publishing catalogs.*

First heard at the 1964-65 New York World's Fair, "It's a Small World" was written by Richard M. Sherman and Robert B. Sherman for the It's a Small World attraction. The simple song became one of the best-known Disney tunes of all time.

WALT DISNEY'S
The Ballad of Davy Crockett

THE SANDPIPERS, MITCHELL MILLER AND ORCHESTRA
From The Disneyland Television Production "Davy Crockett"

As well as songs, narrative recordings of Disney stories were popular in children's record libraries.

In the 1950s, Disney began its own Disneyland line of records, featuring its current films. New versions of its 1930s cartoon classics also appeared.

Disney's entry into weekly television ushered in one of the Studio's greatest song hits— "The Ballad of Davy Crockett."

DECCA presents music from the Walt Disney production
The Three Caballeros

Charles Wolcott, musical director for the South American films, recorded the movies' songs and themes with his orchestra for two Decca 78RPM record albums.

Even Donald Duck, whose vocal abilities wouldn't threaten one tenor (let alone three), was a popular Disney recording star.

Music played a big role on The Mickey Mouse Club, and a line of Mickey Mouse Club Records was quickly produced.

Little Golden Books had an audio counterpart with the introduction of a line of Little Golden Records.

Disney formed its own record label in 1956 to release music from its animated classics and feature films.

Walt Disney Records first released its music in LP and 45 formats. Today the record line continues with cassettes and CDs.

Songs From Walt Disney's **Snow White** AND THE SEVEN DWARFS
with the same characters and sound effects as in the film of that title
VICTOR RECORDS

RCA's Snow White record album from 1938 was the first true soundtrack recording of a feature film.

Award-winning music

Through the years dozens of Disney songs have been nominated for the Best Song Oscar®. Twelve have won, the first being "When You Wish Upon a Star" from *Pinocchio*.

"When You Wish Upon a Star" (1940)

"Zip-A-Dee-Doo-Dah" (1946)

"Can You Feel the Love Tonight" (1994)

Call of the Wild

IN THE LATE 1940s Walt sent a team of photographers to Alaska to document life there, hoping the footage could be made into a movie. From the thousands of feet of film that arrived back at the Studio, Walt put together a documentary featurette about the life of a seal colony on the Pribilof Islands. Although no one, including Roy Disney, thought there was a market for this movie, the first showing of *Seal Island* qualified it for Academy Award® consideration—and it won!

Taking a peek

Seal Island (1948) became the first True-Life Adventure, a series that was to become among the Studio's most honored. The True-Life Adventures concentrated on a world of animals in which man played no part and the Disney cameras provided intimate peeks into animal life that had never been achieved before, fascinating audiences.

Setting a precedent

The first seven True-Life Adventures were featurettes. *The Living Desert* (1953) was the first feature-length entry of the series, and was also the first film to be distributed by The Walt Disney Company's own motion picture distribution division, Buena Vista Distribution Co.

Cameramen devised various disguises to get their up-close and personal shots of wildlife.

A poster of the Oscar®-winning Seal Island.

COMPOSER
PAUL J. SMITH

Making music

Music played an important part in the True-Life Adventure movies. All but three of the films had scores composed by Paul Smith, who wrote entertaining themes for creatures ranging from scurrying leaf-cutter ants to ponderous African elephants.

The African Lion (1955) gave a fascinating look at lions, giraffes, rhinoceros, elephants, and baboons.

...ar...
E LORD
THE
MAZON!

King of Nature's Most Mysterious Swamp!
WALT DISNEY'S
spectacular, New
TRUE LIFE
ADVENTURE

PROWLERS
OF THE
EVERGLADES
The Land that Time Forgot
PRINT BY TECHNICOLOR

Prowlers of the Everglades (1953) gave an insight into the wildlife of the vast, swampy Everglades of Florida.

Adventure books

The True-Life Adventures were so popular that many were adapted into comic books. In Europe, several high-end art books based on the films were published. These were among the most expensive Disney books up to that time.

The amazing life of a South American jaguar was documented in Jungle Cat (1959).

WALT DISNEY'S
Bear Country
A TRUE-LIFE ADVENTURE FEATURE

WALT DISNEY'S
THE AFRICAN LION
A TRUE-LIFE ADVENTURE FEATURE

Bear Country *and* The African Lion *in comic book format.*

Entertaining Documentaries

O F THE 13 movies that comprise the True-Life Adventure series, eight won Academy Awards®, and they are represented below. Winston Hibler narrated them all and his voice endowed each one with a consistent warmth and personality. Hibler had previously worked in the animation story department before becoming a writer and narrator for the True-Life Adventures.

WINSTON HIBLER

SEAL ISLAND (1948)   IN BEAVER VALLEY (1950)   BEAR COUNTRY (1953)

WHITE WILDERNESS (1958)   NATURE'S HALF ACRE (1951)   WATER BIRDS (1952)

The Living Desert
The first True-Life feature gave a wondrous insight into the American desert, and how this seemingly arid expanse teemed with animal and plant life.

The Vanishing Prairie
The second feature, The Vanishing Prairie (1954), *documented animal life in the American West.*

Buffalo roam in **The Vanishing Prairie**

UNFAMILIAR TERRITORY

Before television brought the farthest reaches of the world into viewers' living rooms, the new People and Places series transported audiences to the beautiful mountains of Switzerland, the Moroccan desert, the highlands of Scotland, and other exotic regions. In 1954 *The Alaskan Eskimo* (left), the first entry in the People and Places series, won an Academy Award®.

Disney Enters TV

BY THE EARLY 1950s, television had become a phenomenon that would change people's lives forever. It changed the motion picture industry, too. The magic box was entertaining so many people in their own living rooms that movie theaters across the country were forced to close their doors, and the motion picture studios saw their revenues disappearing. Fearing this powerful competitor, most studio heads wanted nothing to do with it. But Walt Disney saw television as a great opportunity.

The Mickey Mouse Club logo.

Walt was always interested in how things worked. Many of his shows revealed the tricks behind moviemaking and showed how animation effects were achieved.

Operation Undersea *explained how the new movie* 20,000 Leagues Under the Sea *was filmed.*

TV break

Walt realized television could be used to introduce the public to his movies, as well as any plans he had for the future. He first tested television broadcasting with a special entitled *One Hour in Wonderland*, which aired on Christmas Day, 1950.

As easy as ABC

Walt made a deal with the ABC network in 1954 for a weekly television series called *Disneyland*. It helped him obtain financing and gave him the means to reveal his plans for Disneyland Park to his audience. The immediate success of the Disney series helped turn ABC into the major broadcasting company it is today.

The ABC building and logo.

Walt unveils the plans for his revolutionary theme park, Disneyland.

These renderings of proposed plans for space exploration were shown on Man in Space *in 1955—a time when the world was obsessed with space travel.*

Dr. Heinz Haber, seen here with a spaceship model, was the Studio's science consultant.

Man in Space *presented theories about the effects of weightlessness in a humorous fashion.*

More behind-the-scenes secrets are revealed!

Animal man

Walt became a familiar figure to millions due to his role as host of the weekly TV show *Disneyland*. Walt's daughter Diane has said how much her father enjoyed filming his introductions, particularly when animals were involved. His rapport with even the most unruly members of the animal kingdom was remarkable.

Mickey's club

In 1955, the Studio added another hit show to its TV roster, *The Mickey Mouse Club*. It became one of the most popular children's shows of all time. Many of its child presenters, or "Mouseketeers," now have exciting careers in the showbiz world.

The "Mickey Mouse March" was composed by Jimmie Dodd for the Mickey Mouse Club's *opening sequence.*

Fun to learn

Disney's forays into TV production brilliantly combined educational value with excitement. *The High Flying Spy* is an adventure-packed story based on the exploits of real-life balloonist Thaddeus Lowe, and *The Waltz King* is a lavishly filmed biography of Johann Strauss.

THE HIGH FLYING SPY (1972)

THE WALTZ KING (1963)

WALT DISNEY'S OFFICIAL MICKEY MOUSE CLUB

MICKEY MOUSE MARCH
By Jimmie Dodd

60¢

The Mickey Mouse Club introduced an item of headgear that remains a must-have for Disney fans everywhere: Mouseketeer Ears.

In 1961, a new character appeared on The Wonderful World of Color, *the overflowing fount of knowledge Professor Ludwig Von Drake.*

Lady and the Tramp

A "fantasy world" sequence where dogs were the masters and humans the pets was cut from the final film.

THE STORY OF *Lady and the Tramp* dates back to the late 1930s at the Studio, or more correctly, the story of Lady goes back that far. For when the cute cocker spaniel first padded her way across Disney storyboards, she was Tramp-less. Plots were devised, and romances with neighboring dogs were concocted. But none of the storylines held together. Then Walt came across a tale by Ward Greene about a carefree hound called Whistling Dan. Walt asked Greene to prepare a story that brought Dan (later named Tramp) and Lady together.

The dog world

Greene's treatment and the other story ideas developed throughout the 1940s were finally put into a cohesive form by the early 1950s. Centered on the canine world, the film had enormous appeal and became a special Disney favorite for dog lovers everywhere.

Early concept art of Lady and Tramp together in the moonlight.

Some development sketches of Lady.

Animator Frank Thomas credits storymen Joe Rinaldi (seen here) and Ed Penner as finally making the story of Lady and Tramp work.

Surprise!

Lady arrives at Christmas, wrapped like a gift in a hatbox. This was inspired by the way Walt "wrapped" a puppy as a present for his wife Lillian.

SI AND AM

PEG

What a voice!

On the "Disneyland" TV
show *Cavalcade of Songs*, composers Peggy Lee
and Sonny Burke demonstrated how they recorded
Ms. Lee's "Siamese Cat Song" duet with herself as
Si and Am. In all, Peggy Lee lent her vocal skills
to four of the film's characters: Si and Am, Lady's
mistress Darling, and the worldly pooch Peg.

*The traditional song "Home Sweet Home" is
given a howlingly hilarious performance by
the inmates of the dog pound.*

*At first, Lady's
friend Jock doesn't
trust Tramp, but in
the end he helps to
save him from the
dog catcher.*

*The film ends with
Tramp finally
sporting the badge
of trust—a collar
and license—and
settled down to a
life of domestic
bliss with Lady.*

LADY
AND THE TRAMP

The Story of Two Dogs
by WARD GREENE

Literarily speaking

Having adapted so many
of his films from previously
published works, Walt was
delighted that this original
Studio story reversed the
process and appeared as a
novel based on the film.

TONY

Puppy love

In concept it seemed
unappealing—two dogs
slurping spaghetti behind
Tony's restaurant—but this
scene became one of the
most romantic moments in
the history of the movies.

EN CHANTMENT   H—E—R—E   THE NIGHT WILL WEAVE   ITS MAGIC SPELL   WHEN THE ONE YOU LOVE   IS NEAR   FOR THIS IS THE NIGHT AND THE HEAVENS ARE RIGHT   ON THIS LOVELY BELLA NOTTE

Disneyland

IT WAS WALT'S biggest venture, and his biggest risk. To help finance it, he struck a deal with the ABC Television Network and even raised funds by borrowing against his own life insurance. Financial frustrations, construction problems and setbacks were all forgotten on July 17, 1955, when Disneyland was unveiled to its first visitors—and a TV audience. One New York newspaper called it "The Greatest Show Ever Seen on TV!"

Small is beautiful

Arguably the hit of the 1964–65 New York World's Fair, *It's a Small World* was installed at Disneyland in 1966. Children from many nations poured water collected from around the world into the attraction's waterways as part of the spectacular dedication ceremony.

This early concept art for Sleeping Beauty Castle shows its stunning design. Walt once described it as one of the most beautiful castles in the world.

A world of laughter

Walt wanted to build "a source of joy and inspiration to all the world." Indeed, when Disneyland welcomed its first guests it became "The Happiest Place on Earth" for visitors from around the globe.

Sleeping Beauty Castle takes shape. The original cost of Walt's theme park was a then-astronomical $17,000,000.

The bronze statue called "Partners," is a tribute to Disneyland's creator and the mouse who started it all.

The worlds of Disney

Disneyland opened with five themed areas: Main Street, U.S.A. was a quaint idealization of a turn-of-the-century American town; Adventureland gave visitors the chance to board a jungle steamer and explore an exotic wilderness; Frontierland celebrated America's Western heritage; Tomorrowland featured a simulated rocket trip to the Moon; and Fantasyland was where guests could share in the adventures of many a Disney cartoon star.

Fantasyland, as seen in the 1960s, was redesigned in 1983 in accordance with Walt's original concept.

Mickey's Toontown opened in 1993. It's the area where people can actually step inside the houses of Mickey, Minnie, and their friends.

When Tomorrowland was extensively remodeled in 1998, the Astro Orbitor became the new icon at its entrance.

The Changing Face of Disneyland

W ALT PROMISED that, with time, Disneyland would grow and change. In his opening-day speech he said: "Disneyland will never be completed...as long as there is imagination left in the world," and these words can be heard tapped out in Morse code at the Port Orleans train station in Disneyland. In keeping with Walt's philosophy, many areas of the Park have changed through the years. New attractions, such as the *Matterhorn Bobsleds* and the *Submarine Voyage*, were added in the late 1950s, and attractions such as the *Haunted Mansion*, *Indiana Jones™ Adventure*, and *Mickey's Toontown* pushed beyond the perimeter formed by the train tracks that encircle the Park. Fantasyland received a major redesign in 1983, based on plans that had been abandoned when funds ran low during initial construction. However, no land has seen more changes than Tomorrowland. Because the dreams of the future often become the reality of the present, Tomorrowland has gone through two major redesigns since the Park first opened, one in 1967 and the other in 1998.

The Clock of the World, the original icon at the entrance to Tomorrowland, was removed in 1966 when Tomorrowland was redesigned.

Imagineering

WALT DISNEY wanted to entertain Disneyland visitors by enabling them to interact with the characters featured in the attractions. In the 1960s, *Audio-Animatronics®* technology was developed. This made it possible for characters to be animated in an entirely new way—electronically. The most elaborate application of this innovation was in the *Pirates of the Caribbean* attraction, which opened in March 1967.

Movies to moving figures

Many staff members at Walt Disney Imagineering used their background in animation to help them develop the theme park shows. Animator Marc Davis made hundreds of sketches for *Pirates of the Caribbean*, suggesting characters, costumes, gags, and figure animation.

The entire proposed attraction, including the auction scene illustrated above, was built as a miniature set, with figures about 9 inches high, thus enabling Imagineers to view the attraction the same way the guests would see it.

The dreamers and designers of Disney theme parks are called Imagineers.

A buccaneer trio finds its pirate chantey being taken up by a fourth voice.

Seeing eye to eye

Sculptor Blaine Gibson's experience as a Disney animator proved useful when creating the pirates and townspeople. They were then brought to life by *Audio-Animatronics®* technology.

The pirate auctioneer is one of the attraction's most life-like and complicated figures.

"Yo-Ho, a pirate's life for me," sing the raucous crew.

Making them move

Walt Disney and his staff had been bringing two-dimensional characters to life since the 1920s, but *Audio-Animatronics*® technology opened the door for the animation of three-dimensional humans, animals, and objects. For *Pirates*, movements were programmed on rotating cardboard disks (above). Today, Imagineers program the figures using an animation board known as an Anicon (short for Animation Console). The information is then stored and played back digitally.

Visitors to the attraction find their skiffs caught in a crossfire between the bombardment of the attacking pirate ship and the answering volleys from the Caribbean fort.

Sketches of the mayor being dunked show all the energy invested in the animated figures.

The scene is planned as a repeated action, delighting each passing boatload of guests.

First of many

Walt voiced his enthusiasm for the possibilities of *Audio-Animatronics*® figures by saying "we hope we can really do some exciting things in the future." Since the opening of *Pirates of the Caribbean*, many shows have been created for the theme parks using this technology.

Sleeping Beauty

Princess Aurora is named Briar Rose by the good fairies to keep her real identity a secret.

WALT DISNEY WANTED his third feature-length retelling of a classic fairy tale to be the most exquisite representation of the animator's art ever created. To match the splendor of the visuals, Tchaikovsky's famed ballet score was adapted for the movie's songs and background music. The 1959 movie features one of Disney's most memorable villains, the evil fairy Maleficent. Her "gift" to the baby Princess Aurora is that before her 16th birthday she will prick her finger on the spindle of a spinning wheel—and die!

Fairy tales

Princess Aurora has three good fairies to look after her. Unfortunately, despite Flora, Fauna, and Merryweather's attempts to stop Maleficent, Princess Aurora succumbs to the evil curse. The fairies put everyone in the castle into a deep sleep until the spell can be broken by true love's kiss.

For 16 years the fairies raise Aurora in obscurity, keeping her safe from Maleficent's curse.

FLORA   FAUNA   MERRYWEATHER

Amazing transformations

This lavish movie is full of romance, magic, and action! In one of the most spectacular scenes, Maleficent transforms herself into a towering, fire-breathing dragon. She then attacks Prince Phillip, who is hacking his way toward the castle through a forest of thorns to awaken the princess from her slumber.

Maleficent's dark, flowing costume, with its horned headdress and protruding spikes, foreshadows her transformation into an enormous dragon at the movie's climax.

At last the Prince enters Princess Aurora's castle, and the evil spell is broken by a kiss.

The Art of Art Direction

Creating a distinctive style and look for a movie is no easy matter, and there are several things to consider. The film's time period, the required mood, the region of the world to be evoked, even the available film technology—all influence every aspect of a scene's design. Here is a variety of backgrounds from different movies. Each one reflects the underlying theme of the movie it comes from and demonstrates the Disney artists' imagination and know-how.

1937 SNOW WHITE
As a terrified Snow White runs through the forest, she imagines the trees to be menacing creatures.

1948 JOHNNY APPLESEED
Johnny Appleseed's farm was designed in the primitive style of painting that captures the simple life of early rural America.

1942 BAMBI
The forest in *Bambi* appears as a haven for its woodland inhabitants. To achieve this effect the forest was rendered in a soft, comforting style, underlining the story's lyrical beauty.

1940 FANTASIA
An art deco style was chosen for *Fantasia*'s trip to an Olympian paradise. For this fantasy world of Greek gods and goddesses, flying horses, and cavorting centaurs and centaurettes, vibrant colors were used—sometimes with little resemblance to reality!

1959 SLEEPING BEAUTY
Sleeping Beauty was conceived as a medieval tapestry brought to life through animation. The background paintings reflect the strong horizontal and vertical lines found in centuries-old European art.

1999 TARZAN
The jungle home of Tarzan is a timeless haven unspoiled by civilization. Here massive, ancient trees festooned with lianas shelter and protect the jungle's creatures.

101 Dalmatians

101 DALMATIANS IS based on a contemporary children's classic novel, not a fairy tale. So Disney opted for a more modern look, which was achieved by using new technology developed by Ub Iwerks. The result was a film in which characters and backgrounds blended perfectly, setting the tone for one of Disney's happiest outings.

Pencil layouts were transferred to an acetate overlay.

Bold, flat colors were used on the background paintings.

Disappearing doggies

When Pongo and Perdita welcome their litter of puppies into the world, little do they realize the tragic events that are to follow. Their 15 puppies are stolen by the henchmen of wicked Cruella De Vil, who wants to make them into a fur coat. When the police fail to trace the puppies' whereabouts, it is left to the animals both nearby and far away to assist them in the dramatic rescue.

Revolutionary process

Using the patented Xerox process, Iwerks devised a means of transferring the animator's pencil drawings directly onto animation cels, for the first time preserving the spontaneity and liveliness of the animator's performance.

Matchmaking

Not wanting to remain a permanent bachelor like his "pet" Roger, Pongo finds the perfect mate in Perdita. But he needn't have worried, for Roger eventually finds romance with the lovely Anita.

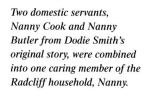

Two domestic servants, Nanny Cook and Nanny Butler from Dodie Smith's original story, were combined into one caring member of the Radcliff household, Nanny.

Clever imagery is used throughout the film. Here, spattered with ink from Cruella's pen, Roger takes on the appearance of his beloved Dalmatian, Pongo.

Twilight bark

Pongo and Perdita use the "Twilight Bark" to send a message to animals in the surrounding countryside that their puppies are missing. The news soon reaches Captain, Colonel, and Sergeant Tibs on a Suffolk farm.

Pencil drawings were transferred to the animation cels and then color was added by hand.

All three stages were combined for the final scene.

Vile, sulfurous smoke curls from Cruella's cigarette—a visible sign of her devilish presence.

ELECTIC Co

Cruella's two shifty henchmen, Horace and Jasper Badun, pose as inspectors from an electric company to kidnap Pongo and Perdita's new pups.

The thought of animating 101 spotted dogs individually was a daunting one! Fortunately, the new Xerox process eased the arduous task.

A vibrant Marc Davis sketch for the flamboyant villain, Cruella De Vil.

Cruel lady

Cruella De Vil is one of Disney's most popular villains. Her gaunt frame, accented by a voluminous fur coat, and her two-tone hairstyle and gravelly voice make her a clever caricature of sophistication, in sharp contrast with the appealing human and canine residents of the Radcliff household.

Mary Poppins

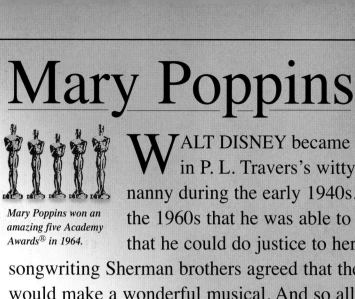

Mary Poppins won an amazing five Academy Awards® in 1964.

WALT DISNEY became interested in P. L. Travers's witty tales of a magical nanny during the early 1940s. But it wasn't until the 1960s that he was able to convince the author that he could do justice to her creation. Walt and the songwriting Sherman brothers agreed that the Mary Poppins stories would make a wonderful musical. And so all the Studio's creative resources were brought together to make a film about a nanny who mends the fabric of a somewhat tattered household.

Mary Poppins' magical umbrella takes her wherever she wants to go.

Making it real

As Walt observed, *Mary Poppins* "would combine cartoon and live action in an enormous fantasy," employing every trick the Studio had learned during 40 years of moviemaking.

Story sketches for the "Jolly Holiday" sequence, which was Disney's most extensive combination of live action and animation to date.

Animator's drawings for the penguins.

Live-action photography of actor Dick Van Dyke prior to its being combined with the animation background.

"Anything for you, Mary Poppins," declare the penguin waiters.

Edwardian England

The original stories were set in England during the 1930s, but the filmmakers changed the time period to Edwardian England (1901–10), adding a quaint charm and color to the film that complemented its storybook appeal.

Don DaGradi's story sketch of nimble chimney sweeps inspired Marc Breaux and Dee Dee Wood's jubilant choreography for the "Step in Time" rooftop dance.

THE PEARLY KINGS AND QUEENS

Super songs

Audiences around the world were carried along with Mary Poppins on her magical umbrella into a musical world full of delightful songs, including "Supercalifragilisticexpialidocious," "A Spoonful of Sugar," and "Let's Go Fly a Kite."

A costume sketch for Mary Poppins. The finished outfit can be seen in the main image to the left.

Costume sketch and swatches for Jane.

A costume sketch for the Bird Woman.

At the end of the movie the Banks family discovers the simple joys of togetherness, thanks to Mary Poppins.

Feed the birds

The Bird Woman was portrayed by Jane Darwell. She was only on screen for a few moments, but her message of caring and charity is at the very heart of the picture. Walt personally chose the veteran actress for this pivotal role, and she came out of retirement for her final screen appearance.

"Feed the birds, tuppence a bag," calls the Bird Woman.

A drawing of the proposed CalArts school that Walt envisioned.

ROY O. DISNEY

Brother To Brother

AS THE mid-1960s approached, Walt Disney was involved in an abundance of projects, from live-action and animated films, to television shows and new directions in outdoor entertainment. Then the world heard the shocking news. On December 15, 1966, Walt Disney died at the age of 65.

Carrying on

After Walt's death, Roy Disney devoted himself to seeing his brother's dreams realized. Significantly, although the Florida Project might have received the name Disney World had Walt lived, Roy wanted it to carry a clear association with his brother and insisted it be called Walt Disney World.

The last animated feature Walt saw through to completion was The Sword in the Stone, released December 25, 1963.

Following Walt's death the Studio continued to produce films in the spirit of its creative founder. One of these, the comedy fantasy The Love Bug, was the highest grossing film in the U.S. in 1969.

From dream to reality

One of Walt's dreams that Roy saw through to completion was The Florida Project's Magic Kingdom and several of its opening day hotels. Roy also carried on the CalArts project, Walt's dream for a school where students of all the arts could come together to study.

Hope and charity

During the last year of his life, Walt continued to lend his personal support and the Studio's resources to charitable and community service projects.

GIVE TOYS FOR TOTS

U.S. MARINE CORPS RESERVE

A poster for one of Disney's many charity appeals.

Winnie the Pooh

WHEN THE STUDIO artists and writers first entered A. A. Milne's timeless and magical world hoping to gather material for an animated film, they hardly realized the incredible impact one "bear of little brain" would have on the Company. Although originally planned as a feature, Walt felt the simple storylines centering on the gentle, bemused residents of the Hundred-Acre Wood better suited featurette length, and so Winnie the Pooh premiered as a Disney animated character in *Winnie the Pooh and the Honey Tree* on February 4, 1966. It was such a success that several featurettes, a TV series, and a movie followed.

Bee-mused
The honey-loving Pooh Bear captures all the gentle innocence and wonder of childhood, making him a favorite of children and adults everywhere.

This scene shows a Shepard-style drawing (recreated by Disney) of Pooh and his friends.

Early concept art shows the Disney artists' desire to capture the look of the Pooh books' original pen and ink illustrations by E. H. Shepard for the films' backgrounds and characters.

Hip hip Pooh-ray!

Christopher Robin and his friends honor Pooh and Piglet, two unlikely heroes of the great flood in *Winnie the Pooh and the Blustery Day*.

Owl leads the way,
All his friends join in, too,
For they're off to a party
For Piglet and Pooh.

Christopher Robin,
Rum-a-tum-tum,
Taps out the march
On his little toy drum.

Mother and son,
Although they are two,
They travel as one,
Missus **Kanga** and **Roo**.

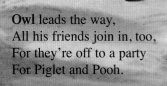

Tigger

The irrepressible Tigger bounced his way into Pooh's life in *Winnie the Pooh and the Blustery Day* (1968).

Eeyore

"Thanks for noticing me." The gloomy old donkey received good notices for *Winnie the Pooh and a Day for Eeyore* (1983).

Piglet

When one is so very small, as timid Piglet often points out, the world can be a very scary place.

Christopher Robin

Author A. A. Milne based the literary Christopher Robin's adventures with Pooh on his own son's imaginative playtimes with his menagerie of stuffed animals.

Cuddly Pooh

As Pooh and his friends were inspired by stuffed playthings, it was only natural that the characters would journey from book to screen and back to toys. In addition to cuddling up with their own Pooh bears, Pooh fans of all ages have made Milne's original creations one of the largest merchandise franchises.

Award-winning bear

Members of the production crew for *Winnie the Pooh and the Blustery Day* gather around the Best Cartoon Oscar® awarded to that film.

Bouncy and trouncy
And bubbling with vigor,
He knows that he's special
'Cause there's only one **Tigger**.

Gloomy old **Eeyore**
Marches with pride;
It's his job to give
The two heroes a ride.

Pooh rescued **Piglet,**
Which was really quite brave (Although it was honey he intended to save).

With gardening tasks
Put aside for a while,
Rabbit joins in
With a prance and a smile.

The Jungle Book

IT MIGHT WELL have been the last Disney animated feature. By the mid-1960s, animated films were proving costly and lengthy to make, and many Disney animators were reaching retirement age. To make matters worse, part way through making *The Jungle Book*, Walt died. However, when released in 1967, this rollicking adaptation of Rudyard Kipling's tale was a triumph, full of hilarious comedy, memorable characters, and delightful song and dance routines. The success of the movie ensured that the legacy of Disney animation would continue.

Artistic inspiration

Sparked by story sketches such as this, the film really started to come together when Baloo's bit role was expanded and his relationship with Mowgli fully developed, becoming the heart of the picture.

Shere Khan

The actor George Sanders lent his coolly urbane tones for Shere Khan, the tiger who wishes to destroy Mowgli, the Man-cub.

Facial expressions for the striped menace are explored (right).

Catchy number

The highlight of the infectious production number "I Wan'na Be Like You" is a duet by Baloo (voiced by Phil Harris) and King Louie (Louis Prima). What makes the moment even more remarkable is that their give and take scat-style banter was recorded during separate sessions.

The vultures

A contemporary note was struck with the chorus of vultures, whose "Beatle-wig" hairstyles and Liverpudlian accents recalled British 1960s pop. They start out by mocking Mowgli, but soon become supportive friends.

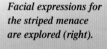

Colonel Hathi

Colonel Hathi leads his elephant brigade on pointless marches through the jungle. Disney favorite Pat O'Malley was the voice of the Colonel in this amusing send-up of a bygone colonial type, the British Raj officer.

Bagheera

Assuming the role of a protective uncle, Bagheera the panther rescues the infant Mowgli from the river and places him in the care of a family of wolves.

Sinister serpent

Actor Sterling Holloway was the voice of Kaa the python. His slyly soothing sibilant sounds served the slithering snake superbly!

Bandleader Phil Harris gave Baloo his laid back vocal style.

Baloo

A carefree bachelor, Baloo nevertheless is so taken with the Man-cub that he wants to adopt him. "You'll make one swell bear!" And for his part Mowgli is only too eager to remain in the jungle with "good ol' Papa Bear."

Pear-picking

Undeniably, the star of the movie was the fun-loving, carefree Baloo. The scene where he picks the prickly pears, during his famous "The Bare Necessities" song is a timeless favorite.

Artist studies for the designs of the apes.

Barbary apes

Realistic studies of Barbary apes helped the animators make the monkeys' movements lifelike and fluid.

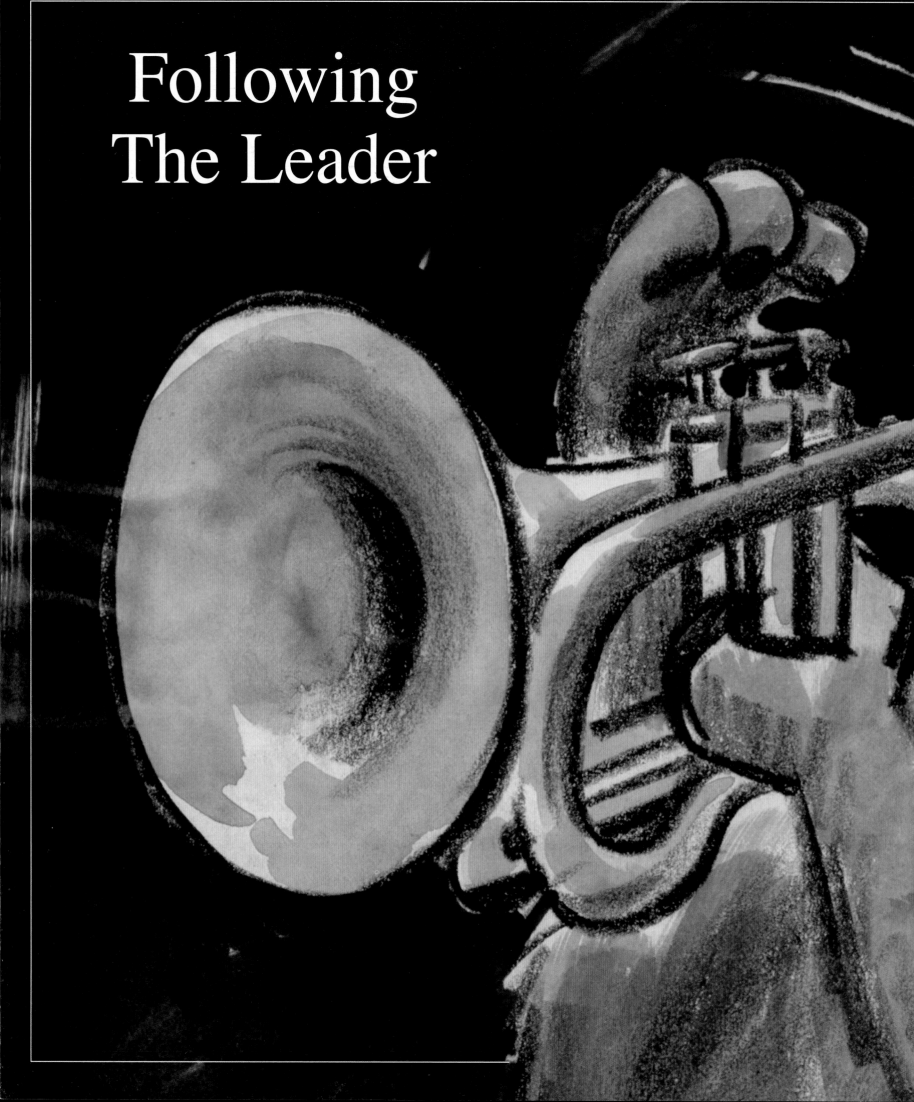

Following
The Leader

W ALT DISNEY HAD acknowledged that his company's accomplishments were due to the combined effort of his team. But there were many who doubted that the talented personnel left behind could carry on the Disney tradition after the loss of Walt's guiding hand.

The Magic Kingdom

Roy O. Disney presides over the grand opening ceremonies at the Walt Disney World Magic Kingdom Park in October, 1971. At its opening, the whole resort had cost a staggering $400 million.

CINDERELLA CASTLE

T HE ELABORATE PLANS Walt Disney had envisioned for The Florida Project were not all realized when the resort opened to the public on October 1, 1971. Still, what *was* there amazed visitors. The resort was full of lagoons, lakes, and golf courses, as well as two resort hotels—the Polynesian and the Contemporary.

And the unforgettable Cinderella Castle standing 185 feet at its center continues to astound thousands of guests even today.

Getting bigger

The Florida resort continued to grow through the coming years, adding additional theme parks, spectacular resort hotels, and a living community where people could make their homes, a central aim to Walt's original vision.

The world famous Space Mountain looms 183 feet above the horizon, beckoning experienced thrill seekers and weak-kneed first-timers alike on a rocket ship ride through the inky blackness of outer space.

Space Mountain in action!

A representation of each newly elected American President is added to the rostrum in the Hall of Presidents attraction.

Imagineers program Henry the Country Bear for The Country Bear Jamboree. This was the first attraction to have its Audio-Animatronics® cast receive new songs, costumes, and patter, enabling them to perform completely different, seasonal shows. The Country Bears were also the subject of a live-action film released by Walt Disney Pictures in the summer of 2002.

Imaginative signage captures the fun of the journey inside Peter Pan's Flight.

On Peter Pan's Flight, guests travel up, up, and away to Never Land in a flying version of Captain Hook's ship, to see Wendy, John, Michael, and the one and only Peter Pan!

Guests get to meet their favorite Disney characters face to face at Mickey's Toon Town Fair.

The Richard F. Irvine, the second paddlewheel steamboat to ply the Rivers of America in Frontierland, was renamed the Liberty Belle in 1996.

Ghouls and ghosts

The exterior of The Haunted Mansion in Florida reflects a Northeastern United States architectural influence, recalling the houses designed by the 18th century wealthy Dutch immigrants. But the ghoulish encounters within are as delightfully frightening as the California attraction, with 999 happy haunts to thrill and scare its guests!

Giant teacups send passengers spinning in a dizzy whirl at the Mad Tea Party.

Designers took full advantage of the lakes and waterways that abound in Central Florida when planning the property's transportation network.

THE HAUNTED MANSION

The Aristocats

MADAME BONFAMILLE

THE ARISTOCATS (1970) WAS the first animated feature produced without Walt's guidance, although it is likely that he gave his approval to the story outline.

Set in Paris at the turn of the century, the film is packed with humor and colorful characters. And even the great French entertainer Maurice Chevalier agreed to come out of retirement to sing the movie's title song. He was happy to do it, he said, "for Walt."

A concept sketch for the jam session...

... and the final finished jazz scene from the movie.

THOMAS O'MALLEY AND DUCHESS

The jazz cats

Music plays an important part in the movie and one of the most memorable scenes is "Ev'rybody Wants to Be a Cat." This uproarious jam session in an attic is performed by an international musical combo composed of the Italian Cat, the Russian Cat, the Chinese Cat, and the English Cat. Several possible songs were written for this sequence, including "Le Jazz Hot" by the Sherman Brothers and "Jazz-Razz-Ma-Tazz" by Terry Gilkyson.

BERLIOZ

Concept art for Duchess's kittens.

TOULOUSE

MARIE

Roquefort the mouse helps O'Malley rescue Duchess and her kittens.

Concept art for Edgar the butler.

Catnapping

The story centers on a pampered mother cat called Duchess and her three kittens, who are abducted by the scheming family butler when he learns they are set to inherit their owner's fortune. But things look up and romance blossoms when Duchess is befriended by an alley cat, Thomas O'Malley, and his gang.

Kidnapping cats can be exhausting, as Edgar soon finds out!

Robin Hood

THE LEGEND OF Robin Hood received a new spin when the Disney artists cast animals as the main characters. Veteran Disney animators, assisted by an outstanding roster of voice talent, including actors Peter Ustinov as Prince John, Terry-Thomas as his fawning sidekick Sir Hiss, Brian Bedford as Robin, and, returning for his third assignment at the Studio, Phil Harris as Little John, helped bring this new version to life.

Little John, Robin's right-hand man and best friend.

A quick-witted fox takes the role of Robin in this action-packed 1973 movie.

Outfoxing the prince

Robin Hood is Sherwood Forest's legendary outlaw, fighting for the rights of the common man (or creature) against the injustices of a cruel regime led by the evil Prince John, his counselor, Sir Hiss, and the Sheriff of Nottingham. Together with Little John, Friar Tuck, and the townspeople of Nottingham, Robin eventually defeats Prince John, returning the country to just King Richard's rule.

Maid Marian gazes wistfully at the hero who is her romantic destiny.

Sir Hiss is suitably servile and ever-willing to further the sniveling Prince John's ambitions.

Concept sketches for the archer baddies.

What a menagerie

Animals didn't have to be native to Sherwood Forest or even the British Isles to be cast in the film. A grinning crocodile archer and an armored rhino fit easily into the film's menagerie of villains.

Ron Miller was determined to continue the legacy of Disney animation. Under his leadership, a recruitment program was begun to train young artists for the animation staff.

Continuing the Tradition

FOUNDED WITH JUST a handful of employees back in 1923, by the 1960s The Walt Disney Company had grown into an international corporation employing thousands of people. Remarkably for an organization of that size, Walt and Roy had managed to maintain a personal involvement in most areas of the Company's businesses. However, some individuals were being groomed to assume full responsibilities when the time came. Sadly, that time arrived sooner than anyone had anticipated.

The Black Cauldron is based on Lloyd Alexander's Newberry Medal-winning series The Chronicles of Prydain.

The new team

When Walt and Roy died within five years of each other, Walt's son-in-law Ron Miller stepped into the creative role for motion picture and television production, also becoming president in 1980. Leading the Company administratively after Roy's death were Donn Tatum and E. Cardon, or Card, Walker.

Animated animals

Several animated movies were put into production under Ron Miller's reign, including *The Rescuers* (concept art above), and *The Fox and the Hound* (concept art left). Development also began on the movie *The Black Cauldron* (concept art top), although the movie was not released until 1985, after Miller's departure.

Elliott is the animated star of Pete's Dragon (1977), an elaborate musical combining live action and animation.

Artwork for the poster of Something Wicked This Way Comes.

The idea for Tron grew from the director's passion for computer games.

State-of-the art computer graphics from Tron.

New movies

In live-action films such as *The Black Hole (1979)*, *Tex (1982)*, *Never Cry Wolf* (1983), and *Something Wicked This Way Comes (1983)*, Ron Miller tried to go beyond the Studio's usual subject matter. This eventually led to him founding Touchstone Pictures.

Concept art for the computerized world of Tron.

Tron

Disney was the leading pioneer in the motion picture industry in 1982 when it released *Tron*, the first feature to utilize computer animation to create a three-dimensional world. This was an appropriate approach for a story set in the world of video games. The movie received Academy Award® nominations for Sound and Costume Design.

1983 MICKEY'S CHRISTMAS CAROL
After a 30 year hiatus, Mickey returned to the big screen in *Mickey's Christmas Carol*. More than 25 Disney animated characters joined him in the Dickens tale.

Animal heroes

THE RESCUERS WAS the first feature that significantly combined the talents of the new members of the animation staff with the experienced artists who had worked with Walt since the 1930s. This transition set the stage for the next movie, *The Fox and the Hound*, which would be handled almost entirely by a new animation team. Many of these new artists had been hand-picked and trained by Disney in the mid-1970s in an intensive recruitment campaign.

The Rescuers

The Rescuers was adapted from Margery Sharp's *Miss Bianca* stories. It tells the tale of two mice, Bianca and Bernard, who set off to rescue a little orphan named Penny, who has been kidnapped by the evil Madam Medusa and Mr. Snoops.

Madam Medusa is a truly memorable villain. Disney ensured that she always had an element of humor despite being a serious threat to Penny.

Early concepts for Medusa ranged from the comically absurd...

... to the darkly sinister!

Medusa's henchman, Mr. Snoops, is a caricature of animation historian, John Culhane.

The Rescuers travel to Penny on Albatross Airlines.

BERNARD

BIANCA

Penny is comforted by Rufus the cat when she despairs that no one will ever adopt her. Disney fans will spot that Rufus is a caricature of animator Ollie Johnston.

Penny struggles to crack the skull that contains the Devil's Eye—the world's largest diamond. Every shot of the scene was carefully planned to build up the tension.

Two early development sketches of the rescue mice, Bianca and Bernard.

The Rescuers was the first Disney animated movie to inspire a sequel. The Rescuers Down Under (1990), takes the intrepid mice to Australia to answer a cry for help.

Talented voices

Part of *The Rescuers* appeal derives from its wonderful voice talent. The Hungarian-born actress Eva Gabor provided Bianca's exotic voice, comedian Bob Newhart was perfect for kindhearted Bernard, and actress Geraldine Page played a suitably evil Madam Medusa.

The Fox and the Hound

This movie follows the story of Tod, an orphaned fox cub, who is raised by a widow living in the country. As a youngster, Tod makes friends with a young hound named Copper. The two grow up, eventually facing each other as enemies, but their bond of youthful friendship wins out over society's dictates.

Rough concept art for Tod's facial and body expressions.

An early sketch of Tod's playful romps in the forest.

Legendary performer Pearl Bailey provided the voice for the sympathetic owl Big Mama.

Part of a series of locomotion studies for a hound dog's running cycle.

Tod and Copper meet as youngsters. The time they spend playing together in the woods establishes the foundation for a believable friendship.

Will it last?

The Fox and the Hound is a story of friendship set against traditional enemy rivalry in the animal kingdom. Foxes and dogs do not normally become friends, but the innocence of youth breaks this rule of nature.

In an attempt to get him out of harm's way, Widow Tweed releases the adult Tod into the forest.

Comic relief is provided by two birds, Boomer and Dinky, and their failed attempts to capture "Squeeks" the caterpillar.

Glen Keane, one of Disney's new young animators, executed the bear fight sequence. Its raw power signaled his potential as a leading animator.

Copper grows up to be a hunting dog—and his friendship with Tod is put to the ultimate test.

Epcot

OPENING IN OCTOBER of 1982, Epcot became the second gated theme park at the Walt Disney World Resort. Major corporations from around the world were asked to participate, and, as a result, Epcot became a showcase for new technologies, as well as presenting a record of mankind's striving for a better life through both industry and the arts.

Past and future

Upon entering Epcot, guests visit Future World, which houses many of the scientific and technological attractions. Beyond Future World lies World Showcase, a section showing the culture, cuisine, and history of many different countries. It also includes American Adventure, which celebrates the American spirit of patriotism, and is hosted by *Audio-Animatronics®* figures of Benjamin Franklin and Mark Twain (above right).

A glimpse of the Global Neighborhood at Spaceship Earth.

In Future World guests can become test drivers on the thrilling Test Track. The ride takes them over bumpy terrain, through hairpin turns, and on to 50-degree banked curves at speeds up to 65 miles an hour!

THE AMERICAN ADVENTURE

World Showcase Pavilions

Gracing the perimeter of World Showcase Lagoon are pavilions representing Canada, the United Kingdom, France, Morocco, Japan, the United States, Italy, Germany, China, Norway, and Mexico. Many young men and women who call these nations home spend a period of time representing their countries at these pavilions, sharing in the experience of international

UNITED KINGDOM

Spaceship Earth

Spaceship Earth is the symbol for Epcot. Assembled like a jigsaw puzzle, it is the world's largest geodesic sphere, comprising more than two million cubic feet of space in which guests travel, viewing examples of man's progress in his need to communicate through language, the arts, and technology. The concept art for the park and Spaceship Earth can be seen above.

FRANCE

GERMANY

JAPAN

NORWAY

MEXICO

ITALY

Tokyo Disneyland

A T THE SAME time Disney Imagineers were designing and building Epcot at the Walt Disney World Resort in Florida, they were also applying their talents to Disney's first international theme park, Tokyo Disneyland. With Oriental Land Company serving as the operating partner, Tokyo Disneyland Park opened on April 15, 1983. The Japanese had admired what had been achieved at Disney's two Magic Kingdom-style parks in the United States, and wanted many of those Parks' attractions recreated for Tokyo Disneyland. Since its Grand Opening in 1983, Tokyo Disneyland has become the most visited theme park and tourist destination in the world!

At Tokyo Disneyland, the 185-foot Cinderella Castle is sometimes magically transformed by a dusting of snow— something unheard of at Disneyland in California or the Magic Kingdom in Florida!

Located within Cinderella Castle in Fantasyland, the Cinderella Castle Mystery Tour takes small groups of guests on an escorted walking tour through the mysterious inner realms of the castle, where they encounter some of Disney's most frightening villains (above).

Herb Ryman's concept rendering of World Bazaar shows how the vast arching glass canopy could protect guests from the weather while framing magnificent views of Cinderella Castle.

CINDERELLA CASTLE

World Bazaar

The charm and atmosphere of small-town America in the early 20th century is recreated in World Bazaar, the first area visited by guests to Tokyo Disneyland. Full-scale Victorian-style buildings house boutiques, specialty shops, restaurants, and *The Disney Gallery*, a showcase for original Disney artwork. The enormous glass-topped canopy, a design unique to Tokyo Disneyland, was inspired by British conservatories of the late 1800s.

Cinderella Castle

The design of Cinderella Castle was inspired by the medieval and renaissance castles of Europe. The famous, turreted castle stands 18 stories tall and is the magical symbol for Tokyo Disneyland.

The design of Splash Mountain (right) is the most spectacular of any Disney park, and has become one of the leading icons of Tokyo Disneyland.

At Pooh's Hunny Hunt guests ride aboard a giant "hunny pot," into the Hundred-Acre Wood for an adventure with Winnie the Pooh, Tigger, Eeyore, and friends.

Guests can step into the wacky world of cartoons in Toontown, where Mickey and Minnie Mouse, Goofy, Donald Duck, Roger Rabbit and other favorites work, live, and play. They can tour Mickey's house and Minnie's house (above) and meet the famous characters.

It's a Small World (left) is featured in every Magic Kingdom-styled Disney park.

The Mickey Mouse Revue

Featuring a cast of more than 40 Audio-Animatronics® stars from some of Disney's most beloved animated films, The Mickey Mouse Revue (above) premiered at the Walt Disney World Resort in the 1970s. In 1983, this one-of-a-kind musical revue moved to Tokyo Disneyland, where it continues to delight guests.

Monster Pioneers

UNDER NEW LEADERSHIP, a fresh burst of energy and optimism infused the Disney organization, along with a determination to develop The Walt Disney Studios into a major Hollywood studio and to venture into areas Walt and Roy had never imagined.

Reaching New Heights

The Horned King invokes an army of undead warriors in The Black Cauldron *(1985).*

WHEN MICHAEL EISNER and Frank Wells came on board in 1984, their first tasks were to evaluate projects currently in production and decide how best to increase company growth and profitability. Almost immediately, a more proactive approach was taken to promoting and developing the theme parks. The company's commitment to live-action television programming was also increased. Two animated features, *The Black Cauldron* and *The Great Mouse Detective*, were completed; and to ensure high standards in future animated films, Disney resolved to scale the heights of excellence it had achieved during its golden age under Walt Disney's leadership.

Many new shows and attractions were added to the theme parks, including Mickey's Toontown Fair.

Mouse genius

The Great Mouse Detective (1986) was a delightful return to animated storytelling. Basil, a mouse Sherlock Holmes, solves crimes using wit and inspired deduction.

Georgette, Dodger, Oliver, Tito, Francis, Einstein, and Rita— the cast of Oliver & Company.

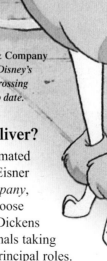

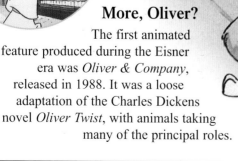

Oliver & Company became Disney's highest-grossing cartoon to date.

More, Oliver?

The first animated feature produced during the Eisner era was *Oliver & Company*, released in 1988. It was a loose adaptation of the Charles Dickens novel *Oliver Twist*, with animals taking many of the principal roles.

To the sky and beyond

The Rocketeer (1991) brought the adventures of Dave Stevens's comic book hero to life in a fun motion picture that harked back to 1930s Hollywood action films. It's a story of an idealistic hero battling a host of dastardly villains with the help of a unique rocket backpack!

Stop-motion animation was employed by director Henry Selick to bring Roald Dahl's delightful fantasy James and the Giant Peach *(1997) to the screen.*

The Rocketeer's poster artwork shows the hero's dramatic lift-off!

The title role in The Santa Clause *(1994) was a perfect fit for actor Tim Allen (right).*

Snow Dogs *became one of the Studio's first comedy hits of 2002.*

Hit series

Disney produced several hit television series, including *Home Improvement*, *Blossom*, and *The Golden Girls*. Despite the popularity of teenage sitcoms, *The Golden Girls* proved to be a real favorite. The show ran for seven years and won an impressive 11 Emmy® Awards!

The series The Golden Girls *starred Betty White, Bea Arthur, Rue McClanahan, and Estelle Getty, and proved that mature members of society could be very entertaining!*

Produced in conjunction with Jim Henson Associates, Dinosaurs *is a prehistoric comedy enjoyed by youngsters because of its wonderful cast of characters and by adults for its amusing send-up of the typical American family.*

Off to Hollywood

TOUCHSTONE PICTURES and, later, Hollywood Pictures, were created to produce more adult-oriented movies. Both had a successful movie program of comedies and dramas, attracting some of Hollywood's top acting and directorial talent. This success, combined with a revitalized and renewed feature animation program, resulted in The Walt Disney Studio leading the way in movie grosses for several years in succession. Not a bad showing for a company that had specialized solely in cartoons a few decades earlier.

Making a splash

Touchstone's first movie was *Splash*, a modern fairy tale about a man (played by Tom Hanks) who falls in love with a mermaid (Daryl Hannah). Released in 1984 and directed by Ron Howard, its popularity with moviegoers marked an auspicious start for the label.

In Down and Out in Beverly Hills, *(1986), Nick Nolte (right), Bette Midler, and Richard Dreyfuss received rave reviews for their performances. But a canine member of the troupe also garnered critical praise. In actual fact, two dogs performed the role, one taking the action shots and the other sharing scenes with the human costars.*

TOM SELLECK STEVE GUTTENBERG TED DANSON
Peter, Michael and Jack know a thing or two about women.
But when it comes to babies, they're all wet.

Three Men and a Baby
They changed her diapers. She changed their lives.

Baby mania

In 1987 it became the highest-grossing Disney movie up to that time. Three Men and a Baby seemed to reach out and connect with thirty-something professionals who were eager to start families of their own.

Julia Roberts and Richard Gere were a winning romantic couple in director Garry Marshall's Pretty Woman *(1990).*

Comic world

Many critics called it the best realization of a comic strip world in the medium of live-action film. Directed by and starring Warren Beatty, *Dick Tracy* (1990) used a stylized color palette in costume and set design to evoke the world of the immortal detective created by Chester Gould.

xt Summer They're Out To Get Him

The Insider

Another powerful true story, this time about the questionable practices of the cigarette industry, found its way to the screen in *The Insider* (1999), which received Best Actor (for Russell Crowe) and Best Picture nominations from the Academy of Motion Picture Arts and Sciences.

Warren Beatty as the comic strip detective hero Dick Tracy.

Arachnophobia

Hollywood Pictures' first release was *Arachnophobia* (1990), a big-budget horror movie based on the near-universal fear of spiders!

The Joy Luck Club

Director Wayne Wang chronicled the lives of Asian-American women in the critically acclaimed *The Joy Luck Club* (1993).

Quiz Show

Quiz Show (1994) takes a look at TV game shows of the 1950s, and explores the scandal that many of them were rigged and their contestants were cheats!

Pearl Harbor

Pearl Harbor (2001) chronicled events leading up to the day the United States was thrust into World War II, and the effects that fateful day had on the lives of ordinary young men and women.

TV Animation

Bumblelion, Eleroo, Moosel, Rhinokey, and Hoppopotamus are The Wuzzles. This odd group of characters live on the Isle of Wuzz!

TO STRENGTHEN Disney's presence in live action and animated television programming, Walt Disney Television Animation was formed to make a series of cartoons. The group created original characters for the first two Disney TV series, *The Wuzzles* and the *Adventures of the Gummi Bears*. Later, classic Disney characters starred in their own series, as did traditional Disney stars such as Donald Duck, Uncle Scrooge, Chip 'n' Dale, Goofy, and Mickey Mouse.

Disney's Adventures of the Gummi Bears related the tales of a clan of bears living in a mythical medieval kingdom.

Inspired by the exciting adventure stories in the Uncle Scrooge comic books, DuckTales sent Scrooge and his grandnephews around the globe on thrilling quests.

Winnie the Pooh's Hundred-Acre Wood was transplanted to television in a series that recaptured the whimsical charm and wisdom of the original movie cartoons.

With their new pals Gadget, Monterey Jack, and Zipper, Chip 'n' Dale became high-spirited Rescue Rangers. Their mission was to fight crime in the animal world.

Bonkers follows the chaotic beat of a recruit in the Hollywood Police Department's Toon division. The feline officer often instigates as much mayhem as he quells.

Cruella and the Baduns crash onto the scene in a typical moment from the 101 Dalmatians television series.

The gang from Recess took a break from the classroom and starred in the theatrical feature Recess: School's Out! (2001)

Pepper Ann *follows the fortunes of an adventurous 12-year-old and her school friends (left).*

Many of the shows produced for television, such as Doug *(left)* showcase a bolder, edgier look than the traditional Disney animation style.

Mickey's MouseWorks, *followed by* House of Mouse, *brought Mickey, Minnie, and all their pals back to the small screen in a big way.*

Chronicling the adventures of its title hero's teenage years, Hercules *follows the young demigod as he confronts a legendary assortment of beasts and villains.*

When you're a talking dog who longs for an education there's only one course open to you: disguise yourself as a boy and end up as the Teacher's Pet.

The TV series Lloyd in Space *premiered in Spring 2001 and follows the adventures of Lloyd the alien and his friends who live on a space station in outer space.*

More movies

Several theatrical features have also been produced by Walt Disney Television Animation. The first was *DuckTales: The Movie, Treasure of the Lost Lamp* (1990), followed by *A Goofy Movie* (1995), and *The Tigger Movie* (2001).

Kiara and Kovu are the stars of The Lion King II *(left).*

Walt Disney Television Animation has also made some popular direct to video features, including The Return of Jafar, The Lion King II: Simba's Pride, *and* Lady and the Tramp II: Scamp's Adventure.

Scamp is the mischievous pup in Lady and the Tramp II *(right).*

Return to Never Land *(2002) is the sequel to* Peter Pan *and was made nearly 50 years after the original movie!*

Disney-MGM Studios

IN 1989, A THIRD gated theme park was unveiled at the Walt Disney World Resort. A celebration of movies and of Hollywood, the Disney-MGM Studios was designed to give visitors a peek at the secrets of moviemaking, as well as a chance to relive fond memories through attractions and shows. The designers set the tone for the day's experience in the buildings lining the park's entry avenue, Hollywood Boulevard, which feature authentic art-deco architectural details from many famous Hollywood landmarks.

Many of the buildings are in the nostalgic art-deco style.

Behind the scenes

Visitors to the park literally step into the world of movies, TV, and animation. They can take a look behind the scenes of filmmaking on the backlot tour, meet the Muppets in *Jim Henson's MuppetVision 3-D*, thrill to the action at the *Indiana Jones™ Epic Stunt Spectacular* and take a ride in an out-of-control space vehicle on *Star Tours*.

The Twighlight Zone Tower of Terror™ houses the most terrifying elevator drop ride ever built, plummeting 13 stories again and again!

Mickey's distinctive gloved hand and sorcerer's hat make a great backdrop for the 100 Years of Disney celebration.

Sorcerer Mickey takes on some wicked villains in Fantasmic, *an action-packed showdown with lasers, lights, fireworks, and amazing "dancing" water displays.*

The Magic of Disney Animation takes visitors to the drafting tables and story rooms of Disney animation.

The thrilling Rock 'n' Roller Coaster *zooms through the world of rock music to the driving beat of the rock band Aerosmith!*

Honey, I Shrunk the Kids!

Youngsters feel no bigger than insects when they enter the play area inspired by the movie *Honey, I Shrunk the Kids*. The entire playground is larger than life, just like in the movie!

The Animal Kingdom

A N ENTIRE theme park dedicated to the wonders of the animal kingdom opened at Walt Disney World in 1998. The park's visual and symbolic center is the Tree of Life, whose massive spiraling trunk and branches feature 325 beautifully carved images of the many different animal species. In addition to the imaginatively designed shows and exhibits, Disney's Animal Kingdom is also home to a variety of wildlife, from lions and tigers to giraffes and elephants!

Disney's Animal Kingdom

Festival of the Lion King is one of several shows that take place at Disney's Animal Kingdom. In it, Simba, Timon, and Pumbaa lead a tribal celebration full of color, joyous Disney music, and special performances.

CONCEPT ART FOR THE
TREE OF LIFE

Kilimanjaro Safari's drivers guide guests through the 110-acre Harambe Wildlife Reserve.

Guests can travel back 65 million years to save prehistoric beasts in the Dinosaur *attraction in DinoLand.*

THE COMPLETED
TREE OF LIFE

Into the wild

Disney's Animal Kingdom Lodge is surrounded by a 33-acre savanna where more than 200 animals roam. A total of 36 species of mammals and 26 species of birds live in the reserve.

The Tree of Life

OWL

The impressive Tree of Life is actually a modified oil rig (six steel columns placed in a circle that rise up to a platform). It stands 145 feet tall and has 325 animal carvings. The animals were carved in plaster and then painted to look like bark. Each creature is amazingly accurate—the detail of the eagle's wing, for instance, took two weeks to carve.

The Little Mermaid

SEBASTIAN THE SINGING CRAB

WHEN WALT'S NEPHEW Roy E. Disney started as Head of Animation at the Disney Studios in 1985, the wheels of change began to turn. Roy and Vice President, Peter Schneider brought a fresh, vital approach to the feature animation division. Working with a talented and enthusiastic staff they ushered in a second golden age of Disney animation, starting with a musical version of Hans Christian Andersen's fairy tale *The Little Mermaid*.

SEBASTIAN

ARIEL

FLOUNDER

Ariel became the first Disney heroine to struggle with parental authority as she tried to deal with her own personal desires and destiny.

Award-winning team

Songwriters Howard Ashman and Alan Menken brought a new approach to the music for *The Little Mermaid*, spicing up the songs with reggae and calypso melodies. "Under the Sea" won an Oscar® for Best Song and the score was awarded an Oscar® for Best Original Score.

Ashman also served as associate producer and was instrumental in character and story development.

Story sketches of Sebastian and some of the ocean residents who perform the fin-tapping, Academy Award®-winning song.

Disney had considered making an animated film of The Little Mermaid in the 1930s, and Danish illustrator Kay Nielsen created concept art for it. This art was retrieved from the archives and used in the planning of the final film.

An actual scene from the film shows the influence of Nielsen's early inspirational work.

When Prince Eric's ship sinks, Ariel rescues him. Always intrigued by the world above the sea, Ariel now discovers she has fallen in love with a human.

Special effects

The Little Mermaid probably had more effects than any animated film since *Fantasia*. Most of the film required some kind of effects work—storms at sea, billowing sails, schools of fish, shadows, raging fire, explosions, surface reflections, underwater distortions, ripples, and bubbles!

Ursula, the sea witch, went through various menacing designs as she slithered her way to her final manifestation.

Ursula's octopus tentacles were reduced to six appendages so that their snakelike writhing could be animated clearly.

A Beast and a Genie

BEAUTY AND THE BEAST (1991) followed *The Rescuers Down Under* (1990). It was an entertainment feast that recaptured the adult audience that had drifted away from Disney animation during the 1970s, and became the first animated feature to be nominated for a Best Picture Academy Award®. The following year, *Aladdin* (1992) confirmed that wit, sophistication, romance, and fun could be combined in a film that truly was for all ages.

The Beast needed to have the appearance of a natural creature, not just a grotesque assortment of animal parts.

Beauty and the Beast

Beauty and the Beast follows the classic tale of a prince who is put under a spell that only true love can reverse. It's a magical feature with lavish scenes and award-winning songs—it won Academy Awards® for Best Song, "Beauty and the Beast," and Best Original Score. In addition, it was the second-ever feature to use the CAPS system. Developed at the Studio, CAPS enabled the artists' hand-drawn animation to be scanned into a computer, where it was then colored and combined with the background paintings.

Glen Keane's early emphasis was on a gorilla-mandrill-type character for the Beast (above).

The evolving design for the Beast took about a year.

The Beast's castle, like its human inhabitants, has been transformed by a magic spell.

Computer-generated imagery was used to enchanting effect for the Beast and Belle's romantic dance in the ballroom.

Lumiere
The Prince's faithful servants continued to serve their master in the guise of familiar household objects.

Cogsworth

Babette

Mrs. Potts

Chip

The servants are destined to remain as objects forever unless they can help the Beast break the spell by loving another and finding true love in return.

Keane's final design for the Beast combined the design elements of a buffalo, gorilla, boar, lion, bear, wolf, and ibis.

Aladdin

The mythical kingdom of Agrabah (left) was the setting for _Aladdin_, a fresh, breezy approach to the retelling of the classic Arabian tale. Tricked into finding the magic lamp by the evil vizier Jafar, Aladdin encounters a powerful Genie, who is required to grant him three wishes. What the Genie finds out, however, is that in Aladdin he has a master who will also make his _own_ wish come true.

Early Genie designs show color exploration and even a Cyclopean influence.

The color choice for the Genie was blue, a "good-guy" color, in contrast to the reds sported by the villain, Jafar.

Aladdin rubs the magic lamp, and releases the Genie.

Jafar uses the power of a magic hourglass to uncover the identity of the "diamond in the rough" (right).

Happy ever after

Eventually Aladdin realizes that Princess Jasmine's love cannot be won by the trappings of wealth and power but by honesty and sincerity (right).

The Lion King

THE RENEWED popularity of Disney animation continued its momentum, culminating in the phenomenal worldwide success of *The Lion King*, released in 1994. The universal appeal of wild animals, coupled with a compelling storyline and rousing musical numbers, resulted in the most successful animated feature ever made. Taking in almost $300 million in the U.S. in its first year, *The Lion King* has become one of the highest-grossing movies of all time.

An African chant heralds the rising of the sun, signaling the gathering of multitudes of animals, set to the song "The Circle of Life."

What a cast!

The movie features a stellar cast of voice talent, including James Earl Jones as Mufasa, Whoopi Goldberg as Shenzi, and Matthew Broderick as the adult Simba. A musical score featuring great songs from Elton John and Tim Rice and background scoring by Hans Zimmer superbly supports the dramatic, humorous, and romantic aspects of the story.

Rafiki the baboon presents the infant Simba to the animals, consecrating him as the heir to Mufasa's kingdom.

SIMBA

TIMON

PUMBAA

Simba's father, Mufasa, guides his cub in the skills needed to be King of the Pride Lands.

This character sketch of young Simba captures his youthful self-confidence and willfulness.

A story sketch of Simba and Zazu the hornbill, who has little patience for the young cub's antics.

Simba's pride

Young Simba's world is turned upside down when Mufasa is killed by Scar, Mufasa's wicked brother. Thanks to Scar, Simba is convinced that his actions caused his father's death, so, guilt-ridden and frightened, he goes into exile. Meanwhile, Scar takes control of the Pride Lands, his incompetent reign turning the savanna into a parched wilderness.

The phrase "hakuna matata" means "no worries" in Swahili and is a maxim for the carefree Pumbaa the warthog and Timon the meerkat.

Simba's sojourn with Timon and Pumbaa introduces him to a jungle life free of responsibilities.

During his stay with Timon and Pumbaa, Simba grows from a fugitive cub into an adult lion.

NALA

Scar is Simba's lifelong enemy. First Scar tries cunning and trickery to get his way, turning to violence when things get tough.

Development art for Scar, the villain of the film.

Scar

Scar plots to overthrow the leadership of his brother Mufasa and the succession of his nephew Simba. Many of Scar's mannerisms, and even his dialogue, were inspired by the accomplished British actor who provided his voice, Jeremy Irons.

New beginnings

The natural order and the circle of life is reasserted at the end of the film when Simba takes his place as ruler of the Pride Lands, with Nala at his side, and their own young cub to ensure the succession.

Disneyland Paris

WITH THE SUCCESS of Tokyo Disneyland, Disney looked toward Europe as the location for its second theme park outside the United States. Construction of the park began in the late 1980s at Marne-la-Vallée, near Paris. But the WDI team was faced with a challenge. Castles are common landmarks to Europeans, so this *Magic Kingdom* had to be *extraordinarily* enchanting. That goal was achieved by enhancing the fairy-tale aspect of the castle and creating one of the most beautiful Disney buildings ever!

Phantom Manor hosts a number of ghosts—predominately the evil "Phantom" and the benevolent "Bride."

Sunny side of Main Street, U.S.A.

Main Street, U.S.A. takes guests back in time to the start of the 20th century, with timber houses, and old-style shops and signs. Visitors can travel from Town Square to Central Plaza in a range of vehicles, including limousines, fire engines, and even horse-drawn streetcars pulled by superb Percheron horses (below).

Mickey and his friends take on a little European style, in classic French berets and colorful shirts!

Main Street, U.S.A. looks fantastic at night (above).

The newest attraction at the Paris resort is Walt Disney Studios Park, which opened in Spring 2002. It's a land of entertainment with four main areas: Front Lot, Production Courtyard, Animation Courtyard, and Backlot.

The Sleeping Beauty Castle featured more fanciful spires and an enhanced color palette than was used for the basically gray stone walls of the existing Disney edifices.

The luxury Disneyland Hotel (right) adds a touch of elegance to the park.

Adventureland (left) has a whole host of attractions, from the oriental bazaar of Aladdin, Adventure Isle with the giant tree from Swiss Family Robinson, and the brand new Indiana Jones™ and the Temple of Peril backwards ride.

Space Mountain in Discoveryland is a 21st-century celebration of 19th-century technology. The most amazing feature of this structure is the 72-feet-long cannon, Columbiad, which takes intrepid space travelers to the top of the mountain in a heart-stopping 1.8 seconds!

Space Mountain, From the Earth to the Moon recreates the daring Moon shot in Jules Verne's From the Earth to the Moon. It is the first Disney high-speed roller coaster ride to have on-board audio. An original score was written by the composer John Debney.

Fairy-tale trees

Even the trees gracing the slopes surrounding the castle have a fairy-tale look, being based on the stylized trees created by Eyvind Earle for *Sleeping Beauty*. A staff of 120 maintains the abundant landscaping at the park.

Disney On Broadway

L ET'S PUT ON a show! The idea received an enthusiastic response at Disney. A source of creative personnel already existed: several members of the animation leadership had Broadway experience, and the theme park entertainment division had been staging live mini-musicals for years. With additional songs by Alan Menken and Tim Rice, *Beauty and the Beast* was brought to the stage. This auspicious start led to one of the most successful musicals of all time, *The Lion King*, and to a third Broadway blockbuster, *Aida*.

The Lion King, New Amsterdam Theatre, New York. Jason Raize as Simba.

Ravishing Renovation

Part of Disney's commitment to Broadway was the restoration of the historic New Amsterdam Theatre to its original splendor. With the assistance of the 42nd Street Development Project, the Disney Company and a team of dedicated architects and restorers spent years restoring the theatre. In 1997 its reopening was celebrated with a concert event, *King David*, readying the theatre to receive Disney's *The Lion King*.

The New Amsterdam Theatre restored to its former glory.

Costume sketch by Julie Taymor.

The Lion King, Lyceum Theatre, London. Paulette Ivory as Nala, Rodger Wright as Simba.

THE LION KING

The Lion King continues to play to sold-out audiences night after night on Broadway. The story of a lion cub determined to discover his place in the world, the show is the proud recipient of numerous citations and awards, including six Tony® Awards and a Grammy® Award. *The Lion King* is currently being produced in cities throughout the world.

AIDA

When Elton John and Time Rice write a musical, Broadway history is certain to be made. With *Aida*, these legendary songwriters have turned the tale of a stolen Nubian princess who falls in love with her captor into a four-time Tony® Award-winning hit musical. With breathtaking sets and costume designs, *Aida* raises the curtain on one of the most powerful love stories in recent Broadway seasons. In addition to numerous other awards, the cast recording of *Aida* received the Grammy® Award for Best Musical Show Album.

Aida captures the contrasting cultures of Nubia and Egypt. (Aida, Fortis Circus Theatre, Scheveningen, Netherlands).

"Elaborate Lives" from Aida, The Palace Theatre, New York. Heather Headley as Aida, Adam Pascal as Radames.

BEAUTY AND THE BEAST

This "tale as old as time" was the catalyst in the Walt Disney Company's decision to devote creative energy to the development of Broadway productions. In this Tony® Award-winning musical, Belle, a young woman yearning for adventure, meets the Beast, who is really a prince under a magic spell. In order to break the spell, the Beast must learn to love another and earn her love in return. With its Academy Award®-winning score, unforgettable characters and eye- popping special effects, *Beauty and the Beast* has dazzled audiences all over the world.

"Be Our Guest" from Beauty and the Beast, The Princess Theatre, Melbourne, Australia.

Costume sketches of Babette and Lumiere by Ann Hould-Ward.

Beauty and the Beast, *The Palace Theatre, New York, Terrence Mann as the Beast and Susan Egan as Belle.*

Sailing in New Directions

T HE GROWTH OF the Disney Company continued throughout the 1990s, taking it into waters previously uncharted by Walt and Roy O. Disney. As well as moving onto the Broadway stage, increasing television production, and opening new theme parks, the Company ventured into the world of professional sports, acquiring a hockey and a baseball team. A cruise line was also established, resulting in the launch of two Disney-themed ships: the *Disney Wonder* and *Disney Magic*.

A Disney-owned tropical island serves as a port of call during the voyage.

THE DISNEY MAGIC
IS AN 83,000-TON
LUXURY LINER.

Wide World of Sports

In connection with the Company's interest in sports activities, Disney's Wide World of Sports opened in 1997 at the Walt Disney World Resort. A state-of-the-art facility for all kinds of athletic activities, it has hosted a variety of amateur competitions as well as serving as the spring training camp for the Atlanta Braves baseball team.

Disney's Wide World of Sports at night.

The Mighty Ducks logo.

A share in the California Angels baseball team, owned by cowboy legend Gene Autry, was acquired in 1996, and the name was changed to the Anaheim Angels.

The Edison International Field in Anaheim is home to the Anaheim Angels. It opened in 1966 and seats 45,500 fans!

In 1992, the Disney Company established a hockey team called The Mighty Ducks. The name was taken from a series of popular live-action comedies, starring the actor Emilio Esteves. As a further tie-in, a half-hour television cartoon series premiered in 1996.

In 1996, the Company acquired ESPN, the major sports network.

Shipshape

Disney's cruise line consists of two luxurious cruise liners. The *Disney Magic* was launched in 1998, and her sister ship, the *Disney Wonder*, followed in 1999. Each can carry a huge number of passengers (2,500 in fact!) and a crew of 950 is needed to look after everyone. The ships have everything a vacationer could wish for, from numerous restaurants, to theaters, fitness centers, and spas.

Goofy gazes out to sea as the ship nears its scheduled stop at Disney's own Bahamian island, Castaway Cay.

Disney's animated stars can be found aboard ship, working and playing—sometimes in somewhat precarious circumstances!

The Little Mermaid statue on the Disney Wonder.

Minnie Mouse's costume has a nautical flair.

In the Animator's Palate restaurant, diners start their hors d'oeuves in the black and white past of early cartoons. But while they are enjoying their meal, their surroundings become more and more colorful!

All aboard

The cabins, restaurants, entertainment, and play areas are all designed to create a unique at-sea Disney experience. And there's a wealth of entertainment for all, from the sports fan to the party lover.

The Secret World of Toys

TOY STORY TELLS OF the magical world of toys who come out to play when humans leave and the doors close. In 1995, Disney co-produced the movie with a young Northern California company, Pixar Animation Studios, making the first-ever feature created solely by computer. No one could have predicted the impact that this feature was going to have; *Toy Story* amazed and delighted the entertainment industry and audiences alike. As a result of this success, Disney and Pixar planned a sequel.

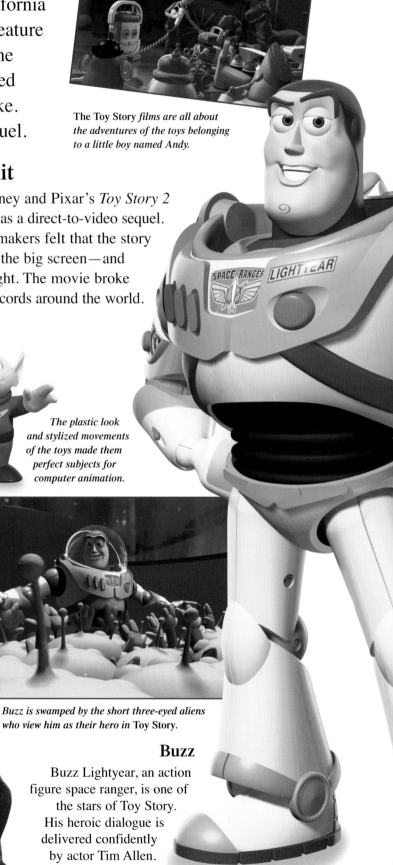

The Toy Story films are all about the adventures of the toys belonging to a little boy named Andy.

Smash hit

Initially, Disney and Pixar's *Toy Story 2* was planned as a direct-to-video sequel. But the filmmakers felt that the story belonged on the big screen—and they were right. The movie broke box-office records around the world.

An early sketch for Buzz captures the confidence that makes him a fitting action toy whose role is to protect the universe.

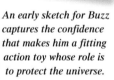

The plastic look and stylized movements of the toys made them perfect subjects for computer animation.

This concept drawing for Woody shows a slight variation from his final costume design.

Buzz is swamped by the short three-eyed aliens who view him as their hero in Toy Story.

REX

Evil emperor

In *Toy Story 2* Buzz finally comes face to face with his archenemy, the Emperor Zurg. But there's a twist, and many an audience member chuckled at Buzz's reaction when Zurg revealed, "I am your father."

Buzz

Buzz Lightyear, an action figure space ranger, is one of the stars of Toy Story. His heroic dialogue is delivered confidently by actor Tim Allen.

Bo Peep is a caring and wise porcelain figure, who holds the key to Woody's heart. She belongs to Andy's younger sister, Molly.

Bullseye is Woody's trusty steed.

Woody is amazed to find out that he was once the star of a 1950s TV marionette show, Woody's Roundup.

Woody

Woody is the leader of the toy gang, voiced with warmth and sincerity by actor Tom Hanks. This doll is Andy's favorite, until a space ranger, Buzz Lightyear, arrives on the scene!

Toy Story 2 *introduced some new toys to the series' toybox, including Jessie the spunky cowgirl doll, voiced by actress Joan Cusack.*

JESSIE

Jessie's crazy critters are always on hand!

Yodelling cowgirl

Like many a TV star, Jessie had her own series of merchandise, including her recording of critter yodels guaranteed to charm the beasts of forest and plains—"Critter Calls."

Bo Peep

Rex

Woody

Zurg

Bullseye

Jessie

Prospector

Mr. and Mrs. Potato Head

Alien

Buzz

Slinky

Hamm

Bugs and Monsters

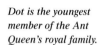

AFTER SOARING to "infinity and beyond" with the landmark 1995 computer animated feature *Toy Story*, Walt Disney Pictures went on to present two more Pixar Animation Studios' films, the box office hits *A Bugs Life* (1998) and *Monsters, Inc.* (2001). These movies brought to life the unusual worlds of ants and bugs, and scary monsters that hide in the closet, with a combination of richly detailed visuals, strong stories, wit, and heart.

Dot is the youngest member of the Ant Queen's royal family.

What a life!

A Bug's Life, an "epic of miniature proportions," is an updated version of the Grasshopper and the Ants fable. Flik and friends try to save their colony from a horde of freeloading grasshoppers.

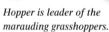

Hopper is leader of the marauding grasshoppers.

"If you believe in yourself, you can do anything," Flik counsels Dot in this storyboard art.

Flik the ant

A Bug's Life stars Flik, an ant whose unusual approach to his work often spells disaster for the colony! Flik proves that he has the makings of an unlikely hero.

Computer graphics enable the movie audience to get a bug's eye view of this beautifully detailed, luminescent world.

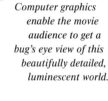

Flik finds himself in a "romantic" entanglement with Atta.

Winged queen

Young Princess Atta has wings, an adornment not bestowed on the average ant. She also has the courage to be a wise and respected leader.

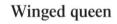

Swat team

Flik invites the circus bugs to the ant colony, believing they are "warrior" bugs that can stand up to the grasshoppers! However, this plan is Flik's biggest mistake.

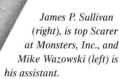

James P. Sullivan (right), is top Scarer at Monsters, Inc., and Mike Wazowski (left) is his assistant.

Scary monsters

Monsters, Inc. enters the shadowy realms inside closets, where monsters emerge to scare children after their parents tuck them into bed. But it's nothing personal—these monsters are just doing their jobs. After all, the main power source in the monster world is the collected screams of children!

Sulley, Mike, and friends all have jobs at Monstropolis's main scream processing plant, Monsters, Incorporated.

It took two years and 30 3-D sculpts to refine Sulley's design. So convincing is his animation that even the almost three million silken hairs on his body quiver with lifelike movement.

Making Boo

Various story approaches were considered for Boo, the little girl who wreaks havoc in the monsters' world. At one time she was spoiled. Then she was bookish. At another she was school age. For a while she wasn't even a she; she was an eight-year-old boy!

An early development sketch of Sulley and Boo. At one time Sulley wore glasses and had tentacles.

Roz

Roz works as the dispatch manager at Monsters, Inc., and like many a person who controls the pulse of a company's operation, she wields unexpected power— and a secret identity!

Door station

The door stations allow the monsters to enter any child's closet. They slide a swipe card coded for each child through the control panel and the correct door is taken from the door vault and slotted into the station. Simple!

Randall

Randall is Sulley's main rival for the top Scarer spot at Monsters, Inc. But creepy, lizard-like Randall cannot be trusted, and he will go to deceptive lengths to secure the position of top Scarer.

Cultural Confrontations

THE SUCCESS OF *The Lion King* persuaded Disney to break away from the traditional fairy-tale themes of their previous films. Director Mike Gabriel suggested telling the story of Pocahontas, even though it meant there might not be the usual happily-ever-after, prince-gets-princess ending. Next they approached Victor Hugo's dark tragedy *The Hunchback of Notre Dame*. In a lighter vein, Disney looked to the Hercules legend—giving it an upbeat, contemporary sound and feel in the movie *Hercules*.

Native Americans served as consultants on the movie to help the filmmakers accurately portray Indian society of the 1600s.

The Hunchback

The Hunchback of Notre Dame (1996) is the story of Quasimodo, a misfit who longs to become part of the world beyond his bell tower. But his evil guardian, Frollo, stands in his way. When Quasimodo does venture into the streets of medieval Paris, he encounters prejudice and hate as well as love and friendship.

Concept art of for "Colors of the Wind".

Meeko the raccoon is Pocahontas's special companion.

The historical Pocahontas enjoyed a close relationship with her father Chief Powhatan, as does her movie counterpart.

Not a happy ending

Pocahontas parts from her lover, John Smith, at the end of the film. Her choice is born of her unselfish desire to maintain peace between the English settlers and the Native Americans. A direct to video sequel was made chronicling Pocahontas's true-life journey to England.

Concept art of Pocahontas by art director Michael Giaimo.

An early development sketch of Quasimodo in his cathedral hideaway.

Although shunned by society because of his ugliness, Quasimodo's inner beauty and worth are recognized by the beautiful gypsy, Esmeralda.

As in the original novel, Notre Dame Cathedral is the focal heart of the Disney movie.

Hades, the ruler of the Underworld, wants to dethrone Zeus and rule the universe in Hercules.

In the original story, Quasimodo talked to the cathedral's bells and stones. So the Disney storytellers fashioned three gargoyles as his friends and confidants.

Disney enlisted British illustrator Gerald Scarfe as Hercules' *Production Designer. His unique styling brought a fresh look to Disney character design and background layout.*

What a myth

Disney's *Hercules* (1997) is a tongue-in-cheek version of the Greek myth. An awkward, yet lovable Hercules is toiling on Earth in an attempt to prove himself to his Olympian father, Zeus. His physical prowess earns him money and fame, but he finds he needs more than these to defeat the jealous Hades and to find love.

Hercules' desire to return to Olympus is only granted when he proves that a true hero is measured by the strength of his heart.

Scarfe's concept of Hercules confronting the vicious Hydra.

A change of life

Hercules is born to Zeus and Hera on Olympus, home of the Greek gods. But his destiny to dwell among the gods is changed when he is kidnapped as a baby and brought up on Earth as a mortal.

Meg is an atypical Disney heroine. Cynical and world-weary, she is redeemed by the innate goodness of Hercules.

Two Legendary Heroes

THE ANIMATED FEATURES *Mulan* (1998) and *Tarzan* (1999) are based on literary sources. While researching China's famed warriors, the Disney team came across a poem about Mulan from the fifth or sixth centuries A.D. Tarzan sprang from the imagination of author Edgar Rice Burroughs, first appearing in print in 1912. Whether historical or fictional, both characters have become very real personalities for the generations that have read about their many adventures.

Mulan feels unsuited for the traditional role of a young Chinese woman.

Mulan transforms herself into a young "male" warrior.

Filmmakers establish a loving relationship between Mulan and her father Fa Zhou.

CRI-KEE

Mulan

The revered woman warrior, Mulan, who fought for her Chinese homeland centuries ago became the subject of a Disney animated feature with an Asian setting. A Disney production team visited China prior to production, gathering inspiration and historical facts for their depiction of one of China's most beloved heroes.

MUSHU

Mulan's two companions, a dragon and a cricket, were inspired by Chinese tradition.

Mulan takes her father's place in the army, not out of a desire for personal glory, but because she wishes to save her father's life.

Shang demonstrates martial arts skills while training recruits for the task of facing the invading Huns.

The evil Shan-Yu is a mean and menacing match for Mulan.

Shan-Yu

Shan-Yu is the ruthless leader of the Huns. He successfully leads his troops across the barrier of the Great Wall of China, defeating the main force of Chinese defenders, and sets off with his army for the Imperial City in order to cause the Emperor's downfall. It is up to Mulan to stop him.

The Legend of Tarzan

Edgar Rice Burroughs' jungle hero had been the subject of countless live-action movies, but the Disney artists knew they could bring something new to the familiar tale. The animators portrayed Tarzan's relationship with his adopted ape family with depth and understanding, and they really shone in their successful depiction of Tarzan as a human with the physical skills, bravery, and loyalty of the jungle animals with whom he lives.

A young Tarzan and his childhood friends.

John Watkiss produced over 80 inspirational paintings of memorable moments from the original Burroughs' tale.

Jane Porter is an adventurous woman who at first finds herself overwhelmed by what she encounters in the jungle!

Energetic line work in early sketches by Tarzan's supervising animator Glen Keane captured the ape-man's strength and agility.

Forced to defend those he loves, Tarzan discovers the real meaning of family.

New technology

Tarzan was made using a new type of technology invented by the Disney designers called "deep canvas." It allows traditionally animated characters to move around in a 3-D world created by computer graphics. The results not only look amazing, but are highly realistic, too.

Tarzan battles a villainess of the jungle, the leopard Sabor.

Fantasia/2000

WALT'S DREAM FOR *Fantasia* was to make it an ever-changing and surprising movie-going experience by constantly developing new musical sequences to replace some of the existing ones. But the movie's disappointing box-office receipts and conditions at the Studio in general during the 1940s meant this dream was not to be... until more than 50 years after *Fantasia*'s release. Roy E. Disney was determined to see his uncle's dream come true. The result: *Fantasia/2000*.

A new beginning

Reminiscent of the abstract visuals created to accompany Bach's 'Toccata and Fugue' in the original Fantasia, Fantasia/2000 opens with bold colors and shapes set into motion by the stirring melodies of Beethoven's "Symphony No. 5."

Wonderful whales

Respighi's "Pines of Rome" was the first new sequence completed. Continuing the tradition of experimentation from the Studio's early years, this sequence utilized computer animation for the free-spirited, soaring whale herd. Only the whales' eyes are executed in traditional hand-drawn animation.

The Rhapsody in Blue *color palette is made up of blues ranging from turquoise to lavender.*

New Yorkers' Rhapsody

Inspired by the design style of caricaturist Al Hirschfeld and the music of George Gershwin, *Rhapsody in Blue* presents a delightfully stylized snapshot of a day in New York. Set in Manhattan during the 1930s, the whimsical tale follows the lives of several diverse characters, including a musician (left).

Concept art for the
ballerina and tin soldier.

A star at last

Like Mickey before him,
Donald Duck finally becomes
the star of his own sequence
in Fantasia/2000, a re-telling
of the Noah's Ark tale set to
several marches from Elgar's
"Pomp and Circumstance."

A yo-yo sets one flamingo
apart from the flock.

Pink flamingos

The finale from Saint-Saëns'
"Carnival of the Animals" is
given a unique look. Both the
backgrounds and characters are in a
vibrant watercolor style, but without
the usual crisp outlines that define the
color areas on an animated drawing.

Tin soldiers

Shostakovich's "Piano Concerto
No. 2, Allegro, Opus 102" is
included in *Fantasia/2000*,
paired with a Studio adaptation
that had been started in the 1940s:
Hans Christian Andersen's
'The Steadfast Tin Soldier'.

Finale

Stravinsky's "Firebird Suite—
1919 Version" concludes the
film. Roy E. Disney was pleased
that thematically this sequence
echoes the original "*Night on
Bald Mountain*"/"*Ave Maria*"
ending, celebrating the triumph
of life over death.

New Grooves

IN THE LATE 1990s Disney established its own group to produce computer-animated films. The first feature made by this group was *Dinosaur* (2000), a journey back to the time when the gigantic reptiles thundered across the Earth. Traditional animation continued with *The Emperor's New Groove* (2000). Disney hadn't explored the terrain of the Incas since the early 1940s, and the Disney team enjoyed the journey into this lively concoction of fun and adventure.

Live-action photography and computer-generated characters were combined in the final movie.

Dinosaurs

The exciting prehistoric adventure *Dinosaur* follows the life of a young iguanodon named Aladar, his life with his adoptive family of lemurs, and his fight for survival against the terrible effects of a giant comet and an evil herd of dinosaurs who spread terror throughout the land.

The young parasaurolophus.

Raised by lemurs, Aladar has an advanced outlook on survival, responsibility, and co-dependency.

Concept art for the carnotaurs—the species of predatory "heavies" in the film.

Dinosaur expressions

The animators had a firm grasp of dinosaur anatomy. However, they found that they had to exaggerate some of the beasts' physical and facial attributes to achieve meaningful and believable storytelling.

KT 009 Ultimate Disney 30

Emperor's New Groove

Kuzco is a spoiled young emperor of a mythical mountain kingdom. Anything Kuzco wants, Kuzco gets. His latest whim is to build Kuzcotopia, his summer getaway—complete with water slide—on a nearby hillside. But his plans are put on hold when he fires his adviser and she plots a rather nasty revenge!

Emperor Kuzco is horrified by his new transformation!

Animal crackers

Kuzco's adviser, Yzma, along with her bumbling assistant, Kronk, plan to poison the Emperor. But it all goes horribly wrong, and Kuzco is turned into a talking llama!

KUZCO

Storyboard art and a final film frame of Kuzco and Pacha's solution to their escape from a canyon's dizzying crevass.

Kronk struggles with the good and bad sides of his conscience.

It is Yzma who turns the arrogant Emperor into a llama!

Yzma

Adviser to the Emperor, Yzma plots to steal the throne for herself. Voiced with delicious villainy by legendary performer Eartha Kitt, Yzma will leave no dastardly deed undone in her quest for power.

The reformed Emperor learns his lesson and decides to do what is good for his subjects— which turns out to be good for him as well.

His spell as a llama teaches the emperor about what really matters in life—teamwork and friendship.

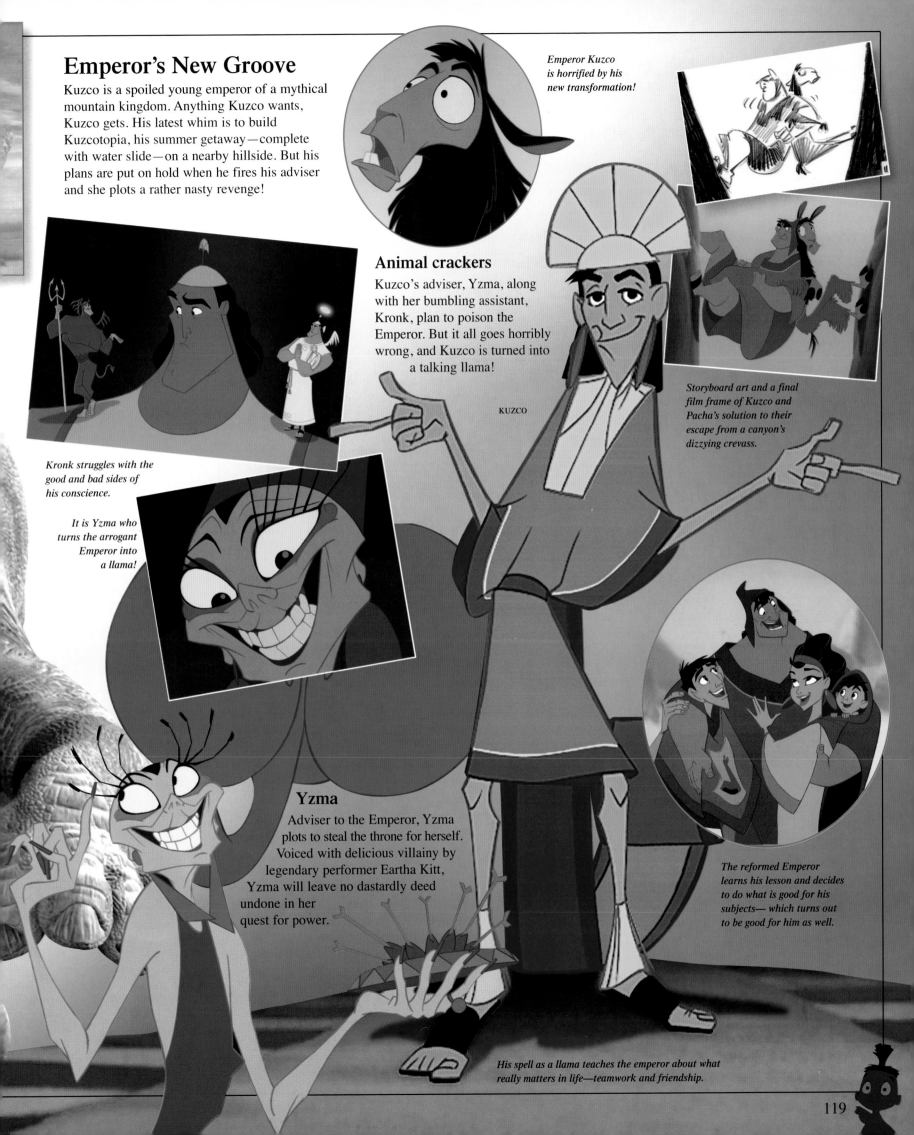

Disney's California Adventure

FUN, EXCITING AND WHIMSICAL, Disney's California Adventure was designed as a fun-filled celebration of California and the California dream, giving guests a unique opportunity to sample the wonders, dreams, beauty, and diversity of California in a Disney world of discovery and entertainment. The park opened in February 2001 and is divided into three thematic areas: The Golden State, Hollywood Pictures Backlot, and Paradise Pier.

Paradise Pier is jam-packed with fun and excitement!

Paradise Pier

Part magical getaway, part nostalgic longing for a bygone era, Paradise Pier promises "Fun in the Sun for Everyone." Guests can zoom from zero to 55 mph in under 5 seconds on the popular roller coaster, *California Screamin'*, or slide in, out, and around the spectacular *Sun Wheel*.

Disney's Electrical Parade combines great music, favorite Disney characters, and thousands of twinkling lights for a magical experience!

Jumpin' Jellyfish (below) takes kids on a fantasy underwater parachute ride.

Hollywood Pictures Backlot

Guests walk through the enormous studio gates of Hollywood Pictures Backlot to discover what appears to be a bustling movie studio. Here, many exciting shops, restaurants, and attractions are found inside sound stages, behind facades or built into movie sets.

Disney's Eureka! A California Parade celebrated the diverse communities of The Golden State.

White-water thrills await guests at Grizzly River Run (above left).

Tokyo DisneySea

TOKYO DISNEYLAND was designed to duplicate as much as possible the look and feel of the Company's American theme parks. But Tokyo DisneySea Park, the second venture with Oriental Land Co. Ltd., is unlike any other Disney park. Located on Tokyo Bay and adjacent to Tokyo Disneyland, it opened in the fall of 2001, and took 11 years to create, from concept to completion. Its seven ports of call invite visitors on an amazing journey into the myths, legends, and lore of the sea.

Near the entrance to the 20,000 Leagues Under the Sea attraction is a 60-foot-high "bubble blurp" (or geyser) water effect that launches more than 32,000 gallons of water into the air.

In Mediterranean Harbor, guests can visit a 15th-century fortress and have a hands-on experience with the Golden Age of Exploration. The volcano towering above the fortress is over 160 feet tall and the biggest man-made rock structure in Disney history.

Island of Mystery

Depicted in this concept rendering is the volcano's hidden caldera known as Mysterious Island. Inspired by the visionary writings of Jules Verne, this place of high adventure allows guests to travel far below the active volcano or even explore a lost city under the sea.

Fantastic realms and unknown dangers await the bold adventurers who set sail on Sindbad's Seven Voyages.

A grand palace is one of the visual delights in Arabian Coast (left) and the Palazzo Canals is one of the enchanting areas of Mediterranean Harbor (below).

Guests can visit Mermaid Lagoon, home to the Little Mermaid and the undersea kingdom of her father, King Triton.

Animated Artistry

Disney's Animation Studio continues to delight audiences with a magical array of films. *Atlantis: The Lost Empire* (2001) follows a journey through the Atlantic's mysterious depths in search of a civilization that sank beneath the sea. *Lilo & Stitch* (2002), set on the Hawaiian island of Kauai, is filled with images of tropical beaches and colorful sea life. Soaring through an imaginary universe, *Treasure Planet* (2002) combines a classic painterly look with a futuristic science-fiction style.

Ulysses, the submarine that carries Milo and crew.

Milo risks his life in a climactic confrontation with Rourke.

Atlantis

Milo Thatch sets out on a quest to prove his grandfather's belief in the existence of the lost city of Atlantis. What he finally discovers defies imagination—a thriving undersea civilization protected by a powerful Crystal force.

Princess Kida lost her mother to the Crystal when a giant wave engulfed Atlantis hundreds of years before. It is Kida's destiny to sacrifice herself to the Crystal to ensure that Atlantis is protected from danger.

Dr. Sweet   Vinny   Milo   Rourke   Kida   Helga   Packard

The crew

Milo's shipmates are a crack team of specialists, ranging from an explosives expert to a geologist to a grease-monkey mechanic. But not all of them can be trusted, as Milo soon discovers.

Cookie   Mole   Audrey

Lilo & Stitch

On a lush Hawaiian island, a lonely little girl, Lilo, adopts what she thinks is a dog. She names him Stitch, unaware that he is the result of an alien genetic experiment. Stitch uses his new identity as a pet dog to evade alien bounty hunters.

Lilo realizes that Stitch's badness level is unusually high, but she is determined to change him. In the end, Lilo's faith in "ohana", the Hawaiian tradition of family, unlocks Stitch's heart and gives him the one thing he was never designed to have—a family.

Watercolors

The filmmakers used watercolor backgrounds to capture the colorful Hawaiian scenery of *Lilo & Stitch* because it created a rich storybook look for the film.

Treasure Planet

Treasure Planet transplants Robert Louis Stevenson's pirate adventure *Treasure Island* into a fantasy space world. The story follows a young man, Jim Hawkins, who leaves home in search of treasure—and finds the treasure within himself.

Solar Surfing

Jim's passion and talent for solar surfing (a combination of windsurfing and skateboarding) prove helpful when he is called to save the crew of the *RLS Legacy*.

An old scatterbrained robot and a protoplasmic shape-shifter are two pals Jim makes on his voyage.

In tribute to the author of Treasure Island, *the filmmakers christened the solar galleon that transports our heroes to Treasure Planet the RLS Legacy.*

Jim befriends the ship's charismatic cyborg (half man, half machine) cook John Silver. But danger lies ahead when Jim discovers that his trusted friend Silver is actually a scheming pirate with mutiny in mind!

The film is an imaginative mix of 18th-century aesthetics and science fiction fantasy.

Jim and Silver look to the stars.

The Future

DREAMING AND FUTURE ASPIRATIONS are very much a part of the everyday work activities of the filmmakers of Walt Disney and Pixar. These two pages feature a sneak preview of just a few of the exciting projects that will reach fruition some time in the future. They all began as wishful "how about this idea" concepts. Yet, after years of painstaking revision, inspiration, and hard work, they will surely earn their place among the memorable entertainment landmarks that have delighted Disney fans for more than 75 years.

Piglet's a star

The shyest and most unassuming resident of the Hundred-Acre Wood seems an unlikely candidate to be the star of a feature film. But in *Piglet's Big Movie* from Walt Disney Television Animation, Pooh and his other friends are happy to discover that Piglet's loyalty, caring, and bravery make him a very special creature indeed.

Finding Nemo

The newest adventure from Disney and Pixar Animation Studios is set in the colorful world of Australia's Great Barrier Reef as seen in these concept art pastels. This voyage of self-discovery and heroism chronicles the eventful travels of two fish—a father and his son Nemo. When Nemo is captured and taken far from home, his father sets out on an epic journey through the ocean to rescue his son.

Bears captures the breathtaking beauty and spectacular natural wonders of the forests of the North American wilderness.

Bears

The artists at Walt Disney Feature Animation Florida are spinning a tale rooted in the lore of many world cultures. Tentatively titled *Bears*, the story follows the adventures of Kenai, a teenager who faces a perilous quest to regain his human form after he is transformed into a bear, a creature he deems his enemy.

Nemo finds himself far from home in a dentist's office fish tank.

The heroines (from left to right): Maggie, Grace, and Mrs. Caloway.

Home on the Range

Some might think the great heroes of America's fabled West are the cowboys or the lawmen. But of course we all know the real hero of the west: the cow. Disney has opened the stable door on these unsung heroes in an hilarious comedy, *Home on the Range*, in which three dairy cows must capture a notorious cattle rustler named Alameda Slim to save their family farm.

The stallion Buck is frustrated about being just the sheriff's delivery horse. A "hero in waiting," he wants to capture Alameda Slim to obtain the glory that has so far eluded him.

Alameda Slim has a secret weapon— an hypnotic yodel that mesmerizes his bovine pursuers.

...ets help ...new friend, ...ng fish

Like any young fish, Nemo is eager to explore the wonders of the ocean.

The Jungle Book II

The Jungle Book II reunites Mowgli with "good ol' Papa Bear" Baloo—one of Disney's happiest pairings. This sequel from Walt Disney Television introduces some new friends for Mowgli from the Man-village, as well as bringing back both friend (Bagheera) and foe (Shere Khan) from the jungle.

Index

Acknowledgments

Dorling Kindersley would like to thank the following for their help in producing this book:

Disney Publishing Worldwide
Margaret Adamic
Rachel Alor
Jack Anastasia
Graham Barnard
Elissa Donenfeld
Natalie Farrey
Brent Ford
Lori Heiss
Hunter Heller
Roger Kaufman
Elliot Kreloff
Tim Lewis
Guido Mastropaolo
Victoria Saxon
Susan Saroff
Ken Shue

Feature Animation
Angela Lepito
Pam Coats
Maggie Gisel
Raphaelle Preynat
Scott Sieffert
Kelly Slagle

Feature Animation Synergy
Kathy Crummey
Holly Macfee
Jodi Sklar

Walt Disney Imagineering
Hugh Chitwood
Dave Fisher
Mike Jusko

Walt Disney Photo Library
Ed Squair

Walt Disney Archives
Brigitte Dubin
Dave Smith
Robert Tieman

Walt Disney Animation Research Library
Doug Engalla
Larry Ishino
Vivian Procopio
Lella Smith

Corporate Legal
Larry Berger
Robert Brogan
Michael Horn
Anne Moebes
Muriel Tebid

Walt Disney World Resort
Darren Chiappetta
Janice Hilliard
Dara Trujillo

Disneyland Paris
Laetitia de Beaufort
Anne-Sophie Thareau

Disneyland/California Adventure
Tari Garza
Christy Holley
Glen Miller

Tokyo DisneySea/Tokyo Disneyland
Sarah Earll

Pixar Animation Studios
Mary Conlin
Krista Swager
Leeann Alameda
Anne Barson

ABC
Coral Petretti

ESPN
Heather Campbell

The Disney Store
Susan Ettinger
Doug Rago

Walt Disney Music
Jonathan Heely

TV Animation
Patty Johnston
Nicole Koshiyama
Penny Milliken

Disney Magazine
David Sokol

Dorling Kindersley would like to thank the following for their kind permission to reproduce their photographs: Whitney Cox (New Amsterdam Theatre, p101), Catherine Ashmore (Nala/Simba, p101), Per Breiehagen (Simba, p101), Joan Marcus (Beast/Belle and Radames/Aida, p102) Brinkhoff/Mögenburg (basket ladies, p102); Anaheim Angels/Lovero Group (Edison International Field in Anaheim, p106).